Exercises in Psychological Testing

Second Edition

Lisa A. Hollis-Sawyer
Northeastern Illinois University

George C. Thornton, III
Colorado State University

Brian Hurd
Colorado State University

Margaret E. Condon
Northeastern Illinois University, Emerita

PEARSON

Boston   New York   San Francisco
Mexico City   Montreal   Toronto   London   Madrid   Munich   Paris
Hong Kong   Singapore   Tokyo   Cape Town   Sydney

Senior Acquisitions Editor: Stephen Frail
Series Editorial Assistant: Katharine Motter
Production Editor: Claudine Bellanton
Manufacturing Buyer: JoAnne Sweeney
Cover Administrator: Kristina Mose-Libon

For related titles and support materials, visit our online catalog at www.pearsonhighered.com.

Library of Congress Cataloging-in-Publication Data

Exercises in psychological testing. – 2nd ed. / Lisa A. Hollis-Sawyer … [et al.].
   p. cm.
Rev. ed. of: Exercises in psychological testing / Margaret E. Condon, Lisa A. Hollis-Sawyer,
   George C. Thornton III. c2002.
ISBN-13: 978-0-205-60989-5
ISBN-10: 0-205-60989-9
1.   Psychological tests—Problems, exercises, etc. I. Hollis-Sawyer, Lisa A. 1963– II. Condon,
   Margaret E. Exercises in psychological testing.

BF176.T47 2009
150.28'7–dc22

                                               2008029392

Printed in the United States of America

10   9   8   7   6   5   4   3   2   1   12   11   10   09   08

EXERCISES IN PSYCHOLOGICAL TESTING
Table of Contents

EXERCISES IN PSYCHOLOGICAL TESTING

PREFACE

The psychological testing course usually takes one of two directions. Some instructors emphasize the measurement aspect of testing, focusing on the processes involved in test development. Others concentrate on exposing students to the range of tests available for various situations and focus on issues of administration and scoring. Both approaches to the course offer students an opportunity to experience concepts firsthand. Theoretically, this means administering and manipulating actual tests. The main deterrent to this is the fact that distribution of many of these tests is restricted, and they cannot ethically be used in the classroom until graduate professional training is taking place. Further, obtaining scores on published intelligence and personality tests can be dangerous without skilled interpretation, and security "leaks" can destroy the value of published tests. In addition, in the undergraduate classroom, the use of published tests does not help in teaching methods of test construction. The study of how tests are constructed helps explain why they are developed in that way, and demonstrates the limitations as well as the strengths of psychological testing.

This manual will provide students with "hands on" experience in various aspects of test development and use. The exercises in this lab manual provide students with opportunities to create tests, administer tests, and analyze test scores. It includes opportunities to give and score several kinds of tests, to construct measurement scales, and to evaluate test reliability and validity. Not all aspects of testing or scoring are represented, but the most important concepts are thoroughly covered in this manual. Further, to keep the exercises to a reasonable length, only samples of test items and/or subtests are presented in each exercise. Important concepts related to testing, such as ethics of testing and obtaining informed consent of examinees, are reiterated across exercises.

This manual could be used in an undergraduate or graduate course in Tests and Measurement or in a freestanding laboratory course in Psychological Testing. Its purpose is to teach understanding of principles through active manipulation and is designed for use in conjunction with any of a number of standard texts in psychological testing. As an exercise manual, it focuses on detailing experiential procedures and frees the individual instructor to decide both the content and the depth of coverage of conceptual material.

The materials and procedures involved in these activities are similar to those used in actual testing situations. It is, however, vital to say that the tests developed by the students or presented in the exercises are NOT valid measures and, thus, interpretation of results is INVALID. Again, the exercises in this manual were designed for the purpose of giving Tests and Measurements students "hands on" experiences in all phases of testing. The authors of this manual believe that this is best achievable through the exercises provided.

Students learn both through reviewing exercise steps and actively applying testing principles by doing the exercises. Data sets are provided for all relevant exercises, allowing exercises to be "stand alone" exercises and not dependent upon the completion of prior, linked exercises (e.g., a later exercise depending upon the completion of the GGAT exercise). This allows flexibility in using the exercises in the lab manual. Up to the discretion of the instructor, a combination of these experiences may be used in each exercise.

For instructors repeating particular concepts through several test types, this lab manual permits them to pick one or more subsets of exercises and still cover the major elements of test development. By including tests modeled on the major tests in each category, those who focus on test surveys have ample opportunities to explore administration/scoring issues in all areas.

The authors of this lab manual realize that instructors and students need to have a lab manual that offers exercises that fit well within the time and coverage constraints of a Tests and Measurements course. To reduce the amount of time in and out of class doing lab exercises, the exercises in this lab manual offer a variety of options for learning testing concepts. There is a great flexibility as to how this lab manual may be used. One way to use the exercises is to have the students take or give the tests in class (developed by the students or provided in the exercise). Having read and experienced the steps in test administration, it is believed that the students will better understand the differences and nuances associated with different testing approaches. Another way to use the exercises for student learning is to have a discussion after reviewing the steps in doing different test development and/or test administration approaches, supplementing lecture materials. Finally, the manual includes data sets associated with most of the lab exercises on the accompanying CD-Rom. Students, after reviewing an exercise, can conduct statistical analyses by using a computer-based statistical program (SPSS) or by hand on the provided data sets on the CD-Rom, or this data can be combined with data collected by the class to judge test score results. Because data sets are provided, the amount of data collected for a class to achieve certain level of statistical power for data analysis purposes has been decreased.

For students, following one test through the development cycle gives an opportunity to use the same material to learn different concepts and, thus, demonstrates the organic relationships among them. The administration of tests is an activity usually enjoyed by students and having their own data to analyze often enhances their motivation to complete the exercises. In addition, we hope that the statistical computations that might not have made sense when first learned will become meaningful when they are put to practical use. Because statistical analyses are necessary for score development, for giving meaning to test results, and for understanding the tests' characteristics, a basic knowledge of descriptive, correlational, and inferential statistics is assumed. We offer in this lab manual support materials to assist the student in doing either hand or computer-based (SPSS) statistical calculations.

In summary, the key features of this second edition manual are that it:

- provides a much more comprehensive coverage of major testing concepts and current "real world" practices (e.g., interviewing, field observation, physical ability testing) through applied, fun, and easy-to-understand exercises, reflecting extensive feedback from both instructors and students in testing and measurement lab courses over the years;

- shows extensive revision of old exercises and the addition of many new exercises to better serve the learning needs of today's college student interested in testing issues and the associated skills to be learned for later application (e.g., graduate school, career preparation);

- is better designed to be more flexible and "user friendly" for instructors who have different emphases in their approach to psychological testing, and can be adapted to courses that differ in length and topic focus (e.g., workplace testing);

- offers improved, easy-to-follow testing exercises reflecting specific test development, administration and/or standardization processes, with an added flexibility of more CD-Rom sample data sets and associated data tables for relevant exercises;

- provides revised templates for charts and tables necessary to better conduct the exercises and lists of materials needed for each exercise, allowing the instructor to more easily focus on content rather than procedural preparation, as well as better optimize student learning; and

- offers better guidance in exercises' steps for conducting statistical analyses either by computer or through manual calculation, with the added feature of more sample data sets on the accompanying CD-Rom to conduct analyses.

Every chart or table is provided. In order to keep the length of the book reasonable, there is usually only one copy of each necessary form. The forms and test materials in the lab manual have perforated edges for easy removal for photocopying purposes.

ACKNOWLEDGEMENTS

The authors would like to thank the people who took the time to be reviewers and editors of the second edition text. From Northeastern Illinois University, the authors would like to thank Lorilene Cuevas and Cristine English for their assistance in reviewing and pilot testing new exercises and revised book content. The authors would also like to thank Erin Crane, Christa Palmer, and Jenny Pitts, graduate students and lab instructors from Colorado State University, who offered numerous suggestions and helped pilot test several of the exercises. Without their help, this second edition would not be as good as it is! The first author would also like to thank Tom and Josh for their wonderful support and understanding during this book revision process.

In memory of:

Dr. Margaret E. Condon, Professor Emeritus, Northeastern Illinois University

A colleague, a mentor, a friend, and much missed!

EXERCISE 1
CODING AND BASIC STATISTICAL PROCEDURES

INTRODUCTION

In order to use the data you collect in many of the exercises, you may have to make it more manageable by creating categories for the data (i.e., "coding" the data). In addition, you will be using basic statistical procedures to analyze that data. In order to review these concepts, this exercise involves collecting demographic data, coding it, and performing some basic statistical analyses either by hand or using a computerized statistical program (SPSS).

MATERIALS NEEDED

2	Copies of the Universal Demographic Sheet (Appendix B)
1	Copy of the Coding Outline
2+	Copies of the Data Sheet (two sides)
1	Copy of the Statistics Summary Tables
1	Copy of the Correlation Data Sheet and Computation (Appendix C)
1	Copy of the Computation of Student's *t* (Appendix D)

✓ If needed, a dataset for coding and statistical analysis is available on the accompanying CD-Rom (*Ex1Data.xls*).

✓ A second file includes answers for the item analysis exercise for the sample data, entitled "*Ex1-ExampleData_Answers.doc.*"

PROCEDURE

Step 1.   *Collect demographic information.*
Each member of the class will complete a Universal Demographic Sheet (Appendix B), and ask one other person to also complete the same sheet.

Step 2.   *Choose variables to code.*
The class will decide on six-eight demographic variables to use in this exercise. Be sure to include some items that could be correlated with other items, and some on which you might want to compare groups of participants with one another. Choose variables that are at each of the four levels of measurement (i.e., nominal, ordinal, interval, and ratio).

Step 3.   *Create a coding guide.*
    a. The class should come to a consensus on which of the variables needs to have categories set up for the answers and what category labels to use when coding the chosen variables. Remember to think about all possible answers you might receive to a given item so that your coding guide is all-inclusive. In addition, some variables may have a large range, and you may want to place the data into meaningful groups. Create a new variable for such a grouped variable (e.g., "AGEGRP") and note what the values represent. For example, the variable "AGEGRP" could have values of "1" (17-21), "2" (22-26), etc.

b. Using this information, now complete the Coding Outline for later use in recording your data. The outline provided here is based on the 11 pieces of information entered in the SPSS Data Editor, but many programs use the same information. **Note**: if you do not plan to use a computer to analyze the data, you will not need the items related to field width or other computer specific information. The content of each of the information sections in your coding guide is as follows:

1. *Item*: The item name as it appears on the Universal Demographic Sheet being coded.

2. *Variable Name*: This is a short name (eight characters or fewer) that is used to identify the variable during statistical operations. It should begin with a letter and may include numbers, but it cannot use any special characters. For example, a usable variable name for "education" might be "Educ."

3. *Type:* This is where you decide whether you are going to enter the data in alphanumeric form (i.e., "string") or number form (i.e., "numerical"). For example, "Sex" can either be coded as "M" for male and "F" for female (alphanumeric) or it can be coded "1" for male and "2" for female (numeric).

4. *Field Width*: This is the total number of spaces the variable required including decimals.

5. *Decimals:* This indicates the number of spaces within the width that come after the decimal point (e.g., 5.62 uses three spaces, 2 of which are decimal places).

6. *Label:* Sometimes you may prefer to have the full name of the variable appear on your lists and output. For example, you may want the variable name "Educ" to appear as "Highest education level" on your output.

7. *Values:* A variable can often be broken into two or more categories (e.g., "Sex" might have two categories: male and female). In this column you will define the values associated with each category. For example, Sex might have values of "1" for male and "2" for female or "M" for male and "F" for female.

8. *Missing:* This column is an accuracy check for your data. In this column you choose a value to use if there is no data and, if appropriate, a value to indicate "refused to answer" or "not applicable." Make sure that the values you use are ones that would never show up as a real value for that variable.

9. *Columns:* This is the total number of spaces you want displayed on the screen. Often it is wise to choose a number that will allow enough of the variable name to show to make it understandable when looking at the screen or data sheet.

10. _Align:_ This column controls the appearance of your data sheet. You decide whether you want the values of a given variable to line up at the left or right margins of the field, or in the center.

11. _Measure:_ This column tells the computer or the statistician what level of measurement is represented by the values of a variable. There are four levels of measurement: nominal, ordinal, interval, and ratio (SPSS calls this level "scale").

Step 4.   _Record data._
Once you have defined the features of your data, you are ready to enter the actual data into the data file or the spreadsheet. In SPSS, go to the "Variable View" screen. If you are doing this exercise by hand, go to the Data Sheets at the end of this exercise. Each <u>row</u> represents all of the data for one participant. Each <u>column</u> represents the data for a single variable across all participants. Refer to your coding guide on how to enter the data. **Note**: If you are using the Data Sheet, you will have to write the variable names at the top of each column. For example, if a participant is female, find the code for that response and enter it into the appropriate column for that person. You should enter information on all of the variables for yourself and the person who completed the Universal Demographic Sheet for you onto the first two lines of the Data Sheet or the first two rows of the database.

Step 5.   _Collate data._
Each class member will share his/her data, so that the rest of the class can complete their Data Sheets or have a complete data file. **Note**: Data for this exercise that may be used for coding and statistical analysis can be found in the companion CD-Rom in the data file "_Ex1Data.xls._" A second file includes item analysis answers for the sample data, entitled "_Ex1-ExampleData_Answers.doc._"

Step 6.   _Compute descriptive statistics._
Each class member will choose four variables and compute the appropriate measures of central tendency (mean, median, and/or mode) and variability (range, standard deviation, and/or variance). Record these answers on the "Descriptive Statistics" section of the Statistics Summary Tables.

Step 7.   _Compute correlational statistics._
Using the Correlation Data Sheet and Computation (Appendix C), each member of the class will compute two separate correlation statistics. For each correlation, choose two continuous variables and calculate the relationship between the two using Pearson's Product Moment Correlation (r). Record these answers on the "Correlation" section of the Statistics Summary Table. **Note**: Choose a value of p and determine the significance of the correlation by using a correlation table or use SPSS to determine the approximate value of p for the correlation.

Step 8.   *Compute student's t-tests.*
Each class member will divide the data set into two groups using one of the variables (e.g., male and female), and will compute the Student's *t* statistic (see Appendix D) to compare the two groups on another continuous variable of interest. Record the answers of the t-tests on the "t-test" section of the Statistics Summary Table. **Note**: Use SPSS or a *t* table to determine the approximate value of *p*.

Step 9.   *Interpret and write-up the results of your statistical analyses.*
Using the Statistics Summary Table, each student will write up the results of the four analyses (two correlations and two t-tests). Each write-up and interpretation of results should be written according to APA style for reporting results. See the examples below:

Sample correlation write-up:

A Pearson Product-moment correlation coefficient (*r*) was calculated to measure the relationship between participants' GPA and number of hours spent studying per week. Results reveal a significant correlation between the two variables, $r(23) = .82, p < .05$, indicating that the number of hours participants spent studying per week was found to be significantly related to participants' reported GPA. As participants spent more time studying per week, GPA tended to increase.

Explanation of sample write-up details:
- *r* indicates that a correlation analysis was performed.
- 23 represents the degrees of freedom.
- .82 is the value of the correlation (*r*).
- *p* indicates whether the value of *r* is significantly different from zero at the .05 significance level.

Sample t-test write-up:

An independent sample t-test was conducted to determine whether there is a difference in the number of speeding tickets received between males ($n = 11$) and females ($n = 14$). Results reveal no significant difference between males and females on the number of speeding tickets, $t(23) = 1.33, p > .05$. The number of speeding tickets reported by males ($M = 3.29, SD = 1.98$) is not significantly different than the number of speeding tickets reported by females ($M = 2.54, SD = 1.36$).

Explanation of sample write-up details:
- *t* indicates that a t-test was performed to compare the means of the two groups.
- 23 represents degrees of freedom.
- 1.33 is the value of *t*.
- *p* indicates whether the two means are significantly different from one another at the .05 significance level.

QUESTIONS

1. How many of your variables reached the ratio level of measurement? Why do you think this is? Which variable was the hardest to code? Why?

2. Did grouping the data seriously change the distribution of any of the variables? If so, which variables? Why do you think this happened?

3. What were the results of your statistical tests? How do you interpret these results? Did any of the results surprise you? Why?

Coding Outline

Item	Name	Type	Width	Decimals	Label	Values	Missing	Columns	Align	Measure
ID										
Sex										
Age										
Age / Group										
Handedness										
Relationship										
Exer. Hrs										
# Speeding Tickets										
Highest Ed.										
Major										
GPA										
Study Hrs										
Working										
Tenure										
Field										

DATA SHEET   **PAGE ____**   **Side A**

Participant #	VAR 1	VAR 2	VAR 3	VAR 4	VAR 5	VAR 6	VAR 7

DATA SHEET   PAGE ____   Side B

Participant #	VAR 8	VAR 9	VAR 10	VAR 11	VAR 12	VAR 13	VAR 14

Statistics Summary Tables

1. Descriptive Statistics Summary Table

Variable	n	Mean	Median	Mode	Range	St. Dev.	Var.
1.							
2.							
3.							
4.							

2. Correlation Statistics Summary Table

Variable	n	Mean	SD	df	r	p
Correlation: 1. Relationship between _____ and _____						
1.						
2.						
Correlation: 2. Relationship between _____ and _____						
1.						
2.						

3. t-test Statistics Summary Table

Group	n	Mean	SD	df	t	p
t-test: 1. Comparing _____ and _____ on _____						
1.						
2.						
t-test: 2. Comparing _____ and _____ on _____						
1.						
2.						

EXERCISE 2
ETHICAL ISSUES IN TESTING: A CASE STUDY ANALYSIS

INTRODUCTION

Both test development and test administration involve being aware of and adhering to ethical guidelines. The American Psychological Association has promulgated a set of ethical principles concerning all aspects of psychological practice, including testing. These ethical principles are designed to protect the dignity and privacy of individuals being tested, and to assure the public of the competence and professionalism of test developers and administrators. They have also published a document explaining the rights and responsibilities of examinees.

Before you engage in any exercises concerning administration or construction of test materials, it is important that you be able to identify and apply ethical issues related to testing. This exercise offers three different case studies, with each case study representing a different issue for class discussion. Each of these presents a situation in which one or more ethical issues are involved. Your task will be to identify the issues involved and how ethical principles were violated, and to suggest ways that the problems might be ethically resolved. This exercise may be completed by the class as a whole or by assigning a different case to each of three work groups.

MATERIALS NEEDED

    1   Copy of each Case Study (#1, #2, and/or #3)

PROCEDURE

Step 1.   *Read background information.*
Before beginning the exercise, each class member should become familiar with one or more of the following:
a.   the chapter on ethics in your assigned textbook, and/or
b.   the documents promulgated by the American Psychological Association. These are available on the web at:
    (1)   www.apa.org/ethics/code.html (the sections on General Principles, General Standards, and Evaluation, Assessment, or Interventions),
    (2)   www.apa.org/science/ttrr.html

The following instructions are written for multiple groups whom each assume responsibility for a single case. If the class acts as a whole, they will repeat *Steps 2 through 4* for each case.

Step 2.   *Read the assigned case study.*
One group (⅓ of class) will be assigned to each case study. Each member of the group will read the case study individually.

| Step 3. | *Analyze the case.* |
| | Using the information obtained in *Step 1*, each group will create a list of what specific ethical issues are involved in the study with citations of the principles involved. |

| Step 4. | *Discover the ethical violation(s).* |
| | The group will create a corresponding list of what occurred in the case that caused the administrators to incur ethical violations. |

| Step 4. | *Suggest possible solutions.* |
| | The group will create, in writing, an alternate scenario that would resolve the ethical problems in this testing situation. Be specific. |

| Step 5. | *Report results.* |
| | Each group will give an oral report to the whole class, which includes: |

a. a synopsis of the case study.
b. the specific ethical issues involved with citation of the principle or standard relevant to the case.
c. the actions in the case that caused the violation.
d. the group's proposed resolution.

QUESTIONS

1. What new thoughts or attitudes have you developed concerning the testing process after reviewing the ethical documents and the case studies? Please be specific.

2. Which ethical case study was the easiest to problem solve? Hardest? Why?

3. How will you approach testing (giving or receiving) differently after doing this exercise?

CASE STUDY #1

The administrator of a long-term care facility is interested in the sleep behaviors of its residents. The administrator holds a staff meeting and informs the nurses and nursing assistants that they are required, in addition to their other shift duties, to administer a "Sleep Survey" to the residents. To best accomplish this, the staff is told to wake up residents early in the morning. This is done to optimize residents' immediate recall of the duration and depth of their sleep. Not seeing any way out of this assigned duty, the staff decides to administer the survey the next morning to all residents. Due to the fact that the staff is far fewer in number than the residents and has other duties to perform before the end of their shift, they decide that the residents need to be awoken beginning at 4 a.m. in order to get it done. The residents, who are mostly groggy and disoriented, dutifully answer the questions posed in order to get back to sleep as quickly as possible.

CASE STUDY #2

A School Psychologist is called into an elementary school to assess the intellectual abilities of a male fifth grader whose grades have slipped from an A average to a B average. Although nervous about being tested, the child is put at ease by the School Psychologist. The resulting scores from a battery of newly-developed, radically-different intellectual ability tests (developed by this same School Psychologist) indicate that the child needs to be removed from the classes he currently takes with classmates and sent to remedial classes. The School Psychologist informs the child's teacher, the principal, and the parents of the child's scores. The School Psychologist emphasizes that only by following the recommendation can the child hoped to be helped.

CASE STUDY #3

The Human Resources Manager of a large corporation is conducting testing of the employees for the purpose of deciding on promotions. Divisions of the company are given different test batteries as related to their differing areas of expertise. Knowing that there is a greater number of older adults in the Sales Division, the Human Resources Manager wants to avoid a potential class action age discrimination suit against the company, and also wants to avoid offending a lot of the salespeople who are close friends. Accordingly, the Manager gives this division unlimited testing time, even encouraging the salespeople to take the test home if needed. Only the Sales Division was paid for their time when taking the test, while the other divisions were not. The Manager limits the other divisions (Manufacturing, Product Development, Advertising, and Product Distribution) to the published time limits associated with their respective tests and to completing them on-site. The Sales Division received five bonus points for "seniority status" when final promotion test scores were tallied.

EXERCISE 3
ADMINISTRATION AND SCORING OF THE
INDIVIDUAL GENERAL ABILITY TEST (IGAT)

INTRODUCTION

The IGAT was designed to teach you about individual intelligence testing without using real test materials. As students, you are not ethically allowed to administer formal intelligence tests but it is important that you understand the processes involved in individual testing. The IGAT includes made-up items that are similar in structure and scoring procedure to those that are part of typical, commercially available intelligence tests.

It is important to emphasize here, again, that the IGAT is not a valid measure of anything. The items on the IGAT were arbitrarily selected, and there are too few of them to function properly as a measuring instrument for either ability or any other type of performance. Because they look like a real test, it is important that you stress to your volunteer participants that this is just an exercise.

This exercise provides experience in giving and scoring individually administered items. There is no way a person can understand or appreciate the challenge of giving a test to an individual or scoring one without actually performing the task.

MATERIALS NEEDED

1	Copy of Informed Consent Form Template (Appendix A)
1	Stopwatch or a watch with a second hand
1	Red pen
1	Sheet blank paper
2	Sharp #2 pencils with good erasers
2	Clean manila folders
1	Copy of the IGAT Administration Manual
1	Copy of each Maze (for use in creating answer keys)
2	Copies of each of the following:

Universal Demographic Sheet (Appendix B)
IGAT Record Sheets
Spatial Relations Sheet
Maze pages (sample maze and two test mazes)
Language Comprehension Sheet
IGAT Behavioral Observations Form

1	Copy of the IGAT Group Data Sheet

PROCEDURE
A.   ADMINISTRATION

Step 1.   *Create an Informed Consent Form.*
The class will create an informed consent form to be given to all volunteer participants that will inform them of the nature and purpose of the exercise, and will reinforce the inability of the items to be a valid measure of anything. Use the template informed consent form template (Appendix A) as a guideline but tailor it to the details of this specific exercise.

Step 2.   *Recruit participants.*
Each class member will recruit two volunteers to take the IGAT, one male and one female.

Step 3.   *Prepare materials.*
For each test to be given, place a Universal Demographic Sheet (Appendix B), an Informed Consent Form, a set of IGAT Record Sheets, the Scoring Guidelines, a Spatial Relations sheet, a set of Mazes, a Language Comprehension sheet, a Behavioral Observations sheet, and an IGAT Individual Summary Sheet in a manila folder.

Step 4.   *Review material.*
a.   Thoroughly review all of the directions for administration that are in the IGAT Administration Manual and the IGAT Scoring Guidelines.
b.   Familiarize yourself with the IGAT Record Sheets.
c.   If you have questions about either test administration or scoring, discuss them in class to ensure that everyone will deal with them in the same way.

Step 5.   *Introduce yourself and the test to your participant.*
a.   Follow the directions in the IGAT Administration Manual for setting up the testing situation.
b.   Have the examinee sign the Informed Consent Form and complete the Universal Demographic Sheet. If the participant declines, thank him/her for his/her time and do not pursue the issue further.

Step 6.   *Administer the IGAT.*
a.   Lay out your manila folder, stopwatch, #2 pencils and red pencil on a work surface that allows the examinee to sit facing you in a room free of distractions.
b.   Open the folder and stand it up to conceal the IGAT Record Sheets and IGAT Scoring Guidelines. Use a good lead pencil for recording verbatim the answers given by the examinee. Erasing mistakes is easier and clearer than is crossing them out.

c.   Administer the six subtests according to the directions and record all answers verbatim on the IGAT Record Sheet, scoring each item as you go along.

d.   After completing all items, thank the examinee and remind him/her once again that the IGAT is not a real test.

Step 7.   *Record observations.*
Immediately after the examinee leaves the room, complete the IGAT Behavioral Observations Form.

B.   SCORING

Step 1.   *Score the IGAT.*

a.   Total the scores for each subtest according to the instructions in the IGAT Administration Manual.

b.   You should end up calculating six total scores, one for each subtest.

c.   On the last page of the IGAT Record Sheet, you will find a section entitled "Summary." This is a summary of all of the person's scores.

   (1)   Enter each subtest total on the appropriate line and then calculate a total "Verbal" score and total "Non-Verbal" score.

   (2)   Finally, by adding up the examinee's total verbal and non-verbal scores, you will calculate a final score for the entire IGAT.

Step 2.   *Record results.*
Copy the raw scores and examinee's ID# for each participant from the IGAT Record Summary to the IGAT Group Data Sheet.

QUESTIONS

1.   What are some specific administrative issues involved when conducting one-on-one testing?

2.   What are some possible confounds resulting from this testing approach?

3.   Which of the subtests were more difficult to administer or score? Why?

IGAT ADMINISTRATION MANUAL

SOME INFORMATION ABOUT THE TEST

The IGAT is made up of sets of items that form six subtests. These six subtests are divided into two groups to measure two classes of behavior called "Verbal" and "Non-Verbal" (sometimes the terms "Verbal" and "Performance" are used). Whether or not tests arbitrarily classified in this way form meaningful measurement groups is an arguable topic but it follows the pattern of the major commercial tests. Be aware that the names given to tests are for the convenience of the examiner. These names do not guarantee that the tests measure what their names suggest.

Verbal:
- I. Information
- A. Analogies
- V. Vocabulary

Non-Verbal:
- S. Spatial Relations
- M. Mazes
- C. Language Comprehension

GENERAL INSTRUCTIONS

The IGAT is to be administered individually to examinees. The personal contact between the examiner and the examinees offers an opportunity for useful observations about behavior that cannot be obtained from group tests.

The IGAT should be administered in a comfortable place, free from noise or other distractions. Use a solid table with ample workspace. Sit opposite your examinee with your materials arranged for quick and convenient access. Allow approximately 30 minutes for each examinee. Follow the administration manual exactly in giving instructions and in scoring the test items.

The directions that are to be read to the examinee are in ***bold italics*** in the Subtest Instructions section of this Manual. Speak clearly and confidently as you administer the test. Conduct yourself in your best professional manner in order to elicit the examinee's best performance.

The directions or questions for most tests may be repeated once but they must be repeated in exactly the same way the second time. Exceptions will be noted in the instructions for particular subtests.

Each subtest has a practice item. Ask that item before you begin the subtest. Explain why the right answer is right even if the examinee answers correctly.

Before beginning the test, put the examinee at ease and establish rapport. Use your own words to make the following points.

1. Thank the person for agreeing to help you with the project.
2. Explain that you want him or her to try to do well but not to worry if some of the questions seem too hard to answer. No one can answer all the questions. *Even though the IGAT is not a test of any characteristic, many people will be concerned about doing well on it. Be sure to explain that the IGAT is only a class exercise and the results have no meaning outside the classroom experience.*
3. Assure confidentiality so that people will feel comfortable if they can't answer an item.
4. State that you will not be able to give the right answers at this time but, if the person desires, you will go over the items later. **Note**: This would not be done with a real test.
5. Ask if there are any questions.

SUBTEST INSTRUCTIONS

VERBAL SUBTESTS

I. INFORMATION

Tell the examinee:

"I am going to ask you some questions about general information. I will repeat each question once."

Read the question exactly as it is on the IGAT Record Sheet. Repeat the question once and once only. Thus, each examinee will hear each question a total of two times. Write the examinee's answers verbatim in the space provided on the IGAT Record Sheet. This is not a timed subtest.

Stop the testing after the examinee gets two consecutive items wrong.

A. ANALOGIES

Tell the examinee:

"I am going to state some relationships. Please tell me what would fill in the relationship to make it as accurate as possible. I will repeat each question once."

Read each item from the IGAT Record Sheet. Each examinee will hear each analogy item a total of two times. Record the answers verbatim in the space provided. There is no time limit.

Stop the testing after the examinee gets two consecutive items wrong.

V. VOCABULARY

Tell the examinee:

"I am going to say some words. Tell me what each word means. I will repeat each word once."

Read the words in order from the IGAT Record Sheet. Say each word clearly. Look up the pronunciation if you do not already know how to pronounce it. Do not spell the word. Repeat each word only once. Thus, each examinee will hear each word a total of two times.

Write the answers on the IGAT Record Sheet as they are being given to you. There is no time limit.

Answer questions by saying one of the following:

"Just tell me what you think the word means." **or** *"I cannot tell you anymore."* **or** *"Tell me what the word means."*

NON-VERBAL SUBTESTS

S.   SPATIAL RELATIONS

With a sheet of blank paper, cover most of the Spatial Relations sheet. Only the sample item should be showing. Place the partially covered sheet and a sharp #2 pencil in front of the examinee. Read the following instructions:

"In each of the lines of boxes on this page, the pictures are from a logical sequence. Four items in the series are given, and you will be asked which of the three choices on the right is the fifth in the series. Your task is to circle the box that you think would be the fifth figure."

"Look at the Sample Item. See how the little squares are moving from the lower left to the upper right. The middle box on the right shows a figure that is higher and more to the right and so would be next in the series."

"Now you complete the rest of these lines. Work as quickly as you can because you will be timed. Tell me when you are finished."

Uncover the test lines and start the timer. <u>There is no time limit but time is recorded.</u>

Stop the timer when the examinee indicates that he or she is finished.

M.   MAZES

Hand the practice sheet titled SAMPLE MAZE and a sharp #2 pencil to the examinee. Read the following instructions.

"Please use a pencil to draw a path through unblocked areas from the ENTER HERE point to the EXIT HERE point. Remember your pencil may not cross any black line."

If the examinee does not make a correct path, take your red pen and draw a correct path, explaining where the mistakes are. If the examinee is successful, proceed with the subtest by saying:

"Now I will give you a series of mazes with each one being a little more difficult than the one before. Complete each maze as quickly as you can because you will be timed. If you make a mistake, erase it and go on. Tell me when you finish each maze."

Give the mazes to the examinee one at a time. Start recording the time for each maze when the examinee gets the maze. Do not wait for the pencil to start because some people visualize their path before they start marking the paper. Stop the timing after each maze is completed. <u>There is no time limit but time is recorded</u>.

Stop the test if the examinee doesn't finish or gives back two consecutive mazes without trying.

C.   LANGUAGE COMPREHENSION

Give the participant a sharp #2 pencil. Using a blank sheet of paper as a cover, place the sheet marked LANGUAGE COMPREHENSION in front of the examinee with only the sample lines uncovered. Say the following:

"In each of the lines on this page, there is a combination of three or more consecutive letters that form a common word. Some read from left to right and some from right to left. Circle the word from each line and then print it in the appropriate place below. When the bottom lines are completed, they will form a meaningful sentence."

"Look at the Sample of three lines. See how two of the words are spelled out from left to right and one is spelled from right to left. They are printed below the three lines and form the sentence PEOPLE LIKE GAMES."

"Now you complete the test lines and sentence. Work as quickly as you can because you will be timed. Tell me when you are finished."

Uncover the rest of the page and begin timing.

Stop the timer when the examinee indicates that he or she is finished. <u>There is no time limit but time is recorded.</u>

SPATIAL RELATIONS

Sample:

Circle One:

 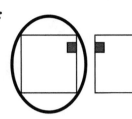

1.

Circle One:

2.

3.

4.

5.

29

SAMPLE MAZE

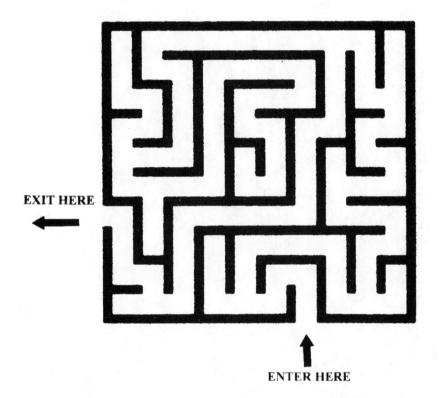

EXIT HERE

ENTER HERE

MAZE 1

EXIT HERE

ENTER HERE

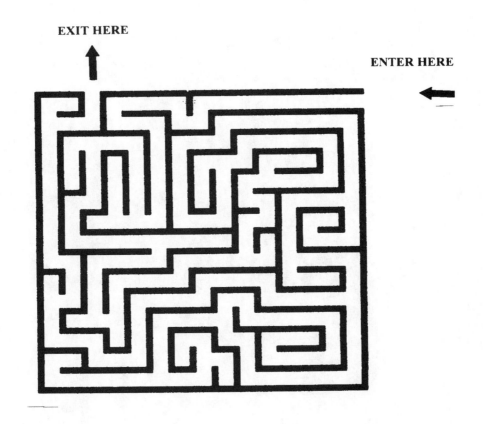

MAZE 2

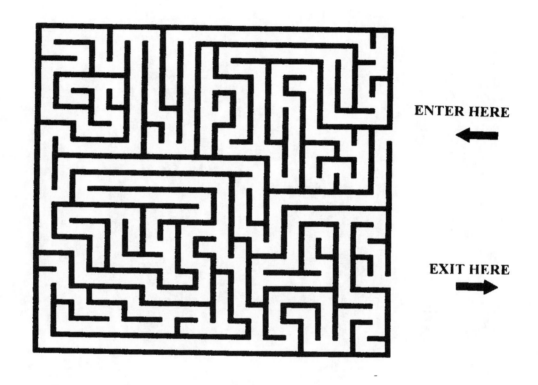

ENTER HERE

←

EXIT HERE

→

LANGUAGE COMPREHENSION

SAMPLE

1.   T F G L A O Q P W T E L P O E P W O F P I S Q T W T G I S

2.   Q O D L I K E G I S L Q T W K G D K S E P H G W I Y K L Z

3.   H D I K S A U E W N C X I G E Q B G A M E S W Q P O M D

Sentence: **PEOPLE**   **LIKE**   **GAMES**
                (First Line Word)   (Second Line Word)   (Third Line Word)

1.   I B G R S S V X I P M R Q T L I O N S L E B W H X O Q P G I

2.   F R L D O J V U L H Q R D N A K N V X A G L T E F T K E X

3.   I M I U Z E B R A S B E Q O T U Z A K F H G T A Z K S M I E

4.   R M N B I Q W V E M O C Y T H L D W N U C N I J R N I Z E

5.   I N Q J E V K F I A H R D F R O M H U Z Y W I P O R X W T N

6.   T I V Z Q L R T D E Q A C I R F A I C M Q D X V Y L W M I W

Sentence: _____   _____   _____
                (First Line Word)   (Second Line Word)   (Third Line Word)

                _____   _____   _____
                (Fourth Line Word)   (Fifth Line Word)   (Sixth Line Word)

IGAT SCORING GUIDELINES

VERBAL SUBTESTS

INFORMATION

Sample: *What are the colors in the American flag?*

Correct	red, white, and blue
Incorrect	any other colors or combinations

1. *How many seconds are there in a minute?*

2	60
1	no partial credit
0	any other number

2. *What is the name of the first book in the Old Testament of the Bible?*

2	Genesis, Book of Creation
1	Pentateuch
0	Exodus, Job, Matthew or any other name

3. *Where is the Liberty Bell?*

2	Philadelphia, Philly, Independence Hall
1	Pennsylvania
0	Washington, New York, Massachusetts, Virginia, Delaware, Boston, etc.

4. *From whom did the United States buy Alaska?*

2	Russia, the Russians
1	Soviet Union, USSR
0	Canada, Europe, France, England, etc.

5. *What is meant by the principle of homeostasis?*

2	balance, equilibrium, keeping things in balance, stability, a constant internal environment, return to resting state, resting point
1	nothing coming in or going out, human stability, state of being
0	things that are alike group together, know what affects one's state, steady pressure, group of elements of an organism, interdependent elements, group of elements

6. *What is a haiku?*

2	17 syllable poem, a 5-7-5 poem, 3 line poem with 17 syllables, Japanese poem of 17 syllables
1	Japanese poem based on syllables, a 3 line poem that captures the moment, a poem with a certain number of syllables, a three line poem
0	Japanese poetry, a Japanese poem, a poem, Japanese verse, 5 line poetry, a country, a traditional Chinese poem, a very short poem, a form of poetry, an island, a poem that does not rhyme, a color, a type of poem, a language, a poem

7. *When was World War I?*

2	1914 to 1918, in the teens of the 20th century
1	early 1900's, early in the 20th Century
0	any other dates in the 20th century, any other century

8. *Where does the term "philosopher king" come from?*

2	Plato's *Republic*, Plato, the Dialogues
1	Greek philosophy, a Greek philosopher, classical philosophy
0	Greek mythology, Freud, Shakespeare, Voltaire, Solomon

ANALOGIES

Sample: *A stocking is to a foot as a glove is to a*

| Correct | hand |
| Incorrect | any other answer |

1. *A floor is to bottom as a ceiling is to*

| 1 | top |
| 0 | other responses |

2. *Bark is to a tree as siding is to a*

| 1 | house, building |
| 0 | other responses |

3. *A wagon is to a car as a bicycle is to a*

| 1 | motorcycle, moped, motorbike |
| 0 | other responses |

4. *A kitten is to a cat as a tadpole is to a*

1	frog
0	other responses

VOCABULARY
Sample: ball

Correct	round sphere used in sports, a formal dance
Incorrect	baseball, basketball, item used in a specific sport

1. *Blunder*

2	stupid mistake, to act stupidly
1	to move clumsily
0	other responses

2. *Opaque*

2	not transparent, light cannot go through it, you cannot see through it
1	not clear
0	other responses

3. *Dominant*

2	ruling, controlling
1	leading
0	game with dots on them, other responses

4. *Summer*

2	the hot season of the year; June 21-September 23 in the Northern Hemisphere
1	one of the seasons
0	no school, other responses

5. *Exotic*

2	foreign, unusual, strange
1	different
0	other responses

6. *Masticate*

2	chew, gnash with teeth
1	soften material
0	other responses

7. *Promulgate*

2	make known, proclaim, teach, put a law into action
1	state an idea
0	other responses

8. *Serendipity*

2	discover something good by accident, fortuitous discovery
1	chance encounter
0	other responses

NON-VERBAL SUBTESTS

SPATIAL RELATIONS
> Score 1 point for each correct choice.

> 1. C   2. A   3. B   4. A   5. B

> If all choices are correct, score points for time as follows:
> | | | |
> |---|---|---|
> | < 30" | = | 3 points |
> | > 31" & < 60" | = | 2 points |
> | > 61" & < 120" | = | 1 point |
> | > 120" | = | 0 points |

MAZES
> Make a set of correct answer mazes by using a red pen on the examiner's set of mazes. Score 1 point for each maze that is correctly completed. In addition, for each completed maze, score points for time as follows:
> | | | |
> |---|---|---|
> | < 15" | = | 3 points |
> | > 15" & < 30" | = | 2 points |
> | > 30" & < 60" | = | 1 point |
> | > 60" | = | 0 points |

LANGUAGE COMPREHENSION
Score 1 point for each word correctly chosen. The correct words in each sentence are:
1. Lions   2. and   3. zebras   4. come   5. from   6. Africa

The complete sentence is: Lions and zebras come from Africa.

Score points for completing the sentence as follows:
    2 points for all 6 words correctly placed in the sentence.
    1 point for at least 4 out of 6 words correctly placed in the sentence.
    0 points if fewer than 4 words are correctly placed in the sentence.

If all words and the sentence are correct, score time points as follows:
    < 60"   = 3 points
    > 60" & < 120"   = 2 points
    > 120" & < 240"   = 1 point
    > 240"   = 0 points

IGAT RECORD SHEET

ID # _____ Examiner_____ Test Date____/____/____

INFORMATION

Sample	Flag: red, white, and blue	Yes	Partial	No
1.	*How many seconds are there in a minute?*	2	1	0
2.	*What is the name of the first book in the Old Testament of the Bible?*	2	1	0
3.	*Where is the Liberty Bell?*	2	1	0
4.	*From whom did the United States buy Alaska?*	2	1	0
5.	*What is meant by the principle of homeostasis?*	2	1	0
6.	*What is a haiku?*	2	1	0
7.	*When was World War I?*	2	1	0
8.	*Where does the term "philosopher king" come from?*	2	1	0

Total_____

ANALOGIES

Sample: hand	*A stocking is to a foot as a glove is to a*	Yes	No
1. top	*A floor is to bottom as a ceiling is to*	1	0
2. house/ building	*Bark is to a tree as siding is to a*	1	0
3. motorcycle	*A wagon is to a car as a bicycle is to a*	1	0
4. frog	*A kitten is to a cat as a tadpole is to a*	1	0

Total _____

VOCABULARY

Sample: Ball	round sphere used in sports, a formal dance	Yes	Partial	No
Blunder		2	1	0
Opaque		2	1	0
Dominant		2	1	0
Summer		2	1	0
Exotic		2	1	0
Masticate		2	1	0
Promulgate		2	1	0
Serendipity		2	1	0

Total _____

SPATIAL RELATIONS

SAMPLE	NS	
Series 1	1	0
Series 2	1	0
Series 3	1	0
Series 4	1	0
Series 5	1	0
Total Time		
Time Bonus < 30 sec. = 3 31 - 60 sec. = 2 61 – 120 sec. = 1 > 120 sec. = 0	3 2 1 0	

Total_____

MAZES

ITEM	SCORE	TIME	BONUS
Sample	NS	0	
Maze 1 Time:	1 0	3	2
		1	0
Maze 2 Time:	1 0	3	2
		1	0

Total _____

LANGUAGE COMPREHENSION

Samples 1, 2, 3	NS
Line 1	1 0
Line 2	1 0
Line 3	1 0
Line 4	1 0
Line 5	1 0
Line 6	1 0
Sentence Completion 6 correct placements = 2 4-5 correct placements = 1 0-3 correct placements = 0	2 1 0
Total Time	
Time Bonus (only if all 6 are correct) < 60 sec. = 3 61 - 120 sec. = 2 120 - 240 sec. = 1 > 240 sec. = 0	3 2 1 0

Total_____

IGAT RECORD SUMMARY

ID#:_____

SUBTEST	TOTAL SCORE
VERBAL	
Information	_____
Analogies	_____
Vocabulary	_____
TOTAL VERBAL (Add subtest scores)	_____
NON-VERBAL	
Spatial Relations	_____
Mazes	_____
Language Comprehension	_____
TOTAL NON-VERBAL (Add subtest scores)	_____
TOTAL SCORE (Add Total Verbal & Total Non-Verbal)	_____

IGAT BEHAVIORAL OBSERVATIONS

ID#:_____

BEHAVIORS DURING TESTING

1. Appearance and posture:

   _____
   _____
   _____
   _____

2. Overall attitude toward testing situation:

   _____
   _____
   _____
   _____

3. Level and kind of emotions displayed:

   _____
   _____
   _____
   _____

4. Approach to tasks that were difficult for participant:

   _____
   _____
   _____
   _____

5. Noteworthy remarks made by participant during testing:

   _____
   _____
   _____
   _____

6. Level of satisfaction expressed about performance:

   _____
   _____
   _____
   _____

7. Additional comments:

   _____
   _____
   _____
   _____

IGAT GROUP DATA SHEET

The total (raw) scores to be recorded here are to be copied from the IGAT Record Summary for each examinee. They are called "raw scores" because nothing has yet been done to them (i.e., score conversion).

ID # of participant		
SUBTEST	TOTAL (RAW) SCORES	
Information		
Analogies		
Vocabulary		
TOTAL VERBAL		
Spatial Relations		
Mazes		
Language Comprehension		
TOTAL NON-VERBAL		
GRAND TOTAL		

EXERCISE 4

ADMINISTERING AND SCORING A
GROUP GENERAL ABILITY TEST (GGAT)

INTRODUCTION

The GGAT was designed to teach about group intelligence testing without having to use test materials that are highly confidential. It includes many of the components of typical commercially available intelligence tests to illustrate what they are like. As was true of the IGAT, the GGAT is an exercise in administration and scoring procedures and not a true test of intelligence or anything else. The items on the GGAT were also not appropriately selected and, in addition, there are too few of them to function properly as a measuring instrument for intelligence. Just as in the IGAT, the items are designed to mimic two classes of behavior called "verbal" and "non-verbal." Whether or not items arbitrarily classified in this way form meaningful measurement groups is an arguable topic but dividing them this way follows the pattern of the major commercial tests.

This assignment involves the administration and scoring of the Group General Ability Test (GGAT) to male and female adults who are at least 18 years old. Try to test at least one person who took the IGAT for you. Remember to emphasize to your examinees that this is not a real test.

MATERIALS NEEDED

1	Copy of the Informed Consent Form Template (Appendix A)
3	Copies of the Universal Demographic Sheet (Appendix B)
6	Sharpened #2 pencils
1	Copy of the Script for Administration of the GGAT
3	Copies of the Group General Ability Test (GGAT)
1	Copy of the GGAT Answer Key
1+	Copies of the GGAT Summary Data Sheet (each sheet holds data for 20 class members)
1	Copy of the GGAT Norms Table
1	Copy IGAT scores for the participants who took IGAT as well
1	Copy of the Correlation Data Sheet and Computation (Appendix C)

PROCEDURE

Step 1. *Create an Informed Consent Form.*
The class will create an informed consent form to be given to all volunteer participants that will inform them of the nature and purpose of the exercise and will reinforce the inability of the items to be a valid measure of anything. Use the template informed consent form as a guideline (Appendix A) but tailor it to the details of this specific exercise.

Step 2. *Select participants.*
Each class member will recruit three persons, of whom at least one person also took the IGAT (Exercise #3). You will be testing them as a group.

Step 3.	*Review the standard instructions.*
	Review and familiarize yourself with the script for GGAT administration.

Step 4.	*Prepare test materials and the testing situation.*

    a.   Put three sets of the following sheets in order, from top to bottom:

        (1)   created Informed Consent Form,

        (2)   the Universal Demographic Sheet (Appendix B), and

        (3)   the Group General Ability Tests (GGAT).

    b.   Assign a random ID number to each participant, and put this number in the appropriate space on both the Universal Demographic Sheet and the Test Form. For those who took the IGAT, use the same ID number you used in Exercise #3 to make comparisons easier.

    c.   Select a testing site that is:

        (1)   quiet and relatively distraction free, and

        (2)   allows for large spaces between participants.

    d.   Place a set of materials and a pencil at the place where each participant will sit.

    e.   Place extra pencils on the table.

Step 5.	*Introduce task.*

    a.   Using the GGAT administration script, introduce yourself and the purpose of the session.

    b.   Ask participants to complete the created Informed Consent Form.

    c.   Ask participants to complete the Universal Demographic Sheet.

    d.   Ask participants to begin the GGAT.

    e.   Allow participants as much time as necessary to complete the test.

Step 6.	*Score the GGAT.*
	Score each completed GGAT using the GGAT Answer Key. Place a check (√) next to each correct answer. On the last page of the test, add up the number of correct answers and place this sum at the bottom of the page.

Step 7.	*Collate data.*

    a.   Copy the total score for each of your participants to the first line of the GGAT Summary Data Sheet. Put the people who took the IGAT in the last column.

    b.   Place an asterisk (*) next to those scores of people who took the IGAT.

    c.   Share your data with the rest of the class, following the same format of putting the "IGAT also" examinee in the last column.

Step 8.   *Create data sets for analysis.*
Using the GGAT Summary Data Sheets, each class member will consider the following two different data sets:

a.   scores for all participants (both those who did and did not take the IGAT), and

b.   scores for all participants who also took the IGAT.

Step 9.   *Calculate standard scores for GGAT.*
Using the scores from all participants (*Step 8*a), compute the following and put into the GGAT Norms Table (use Table of Normal Curve to compute percentiles (%) from z-scores):

a.   mean and standard deviation.

b.   standard scores:

(1)   z scores.

(2)   T scores.

(3)   percentile (% ile) scores.

Step 10.   *Correlate IGAT and GGAT scores.*
Using the data set of those participants who took both tests (*Step 8*b) and the Correlation Data Sheet and Computation (Appendix C), compute the Pearson Product-moment correlation coefficient (*r*) between the Total # Right on the GGAT and the Total (Raw) Score on the IGAT.

Step 11.   *Interpret individual scores.*
Each student will select two of his or her own three participants. **Note**: One participant should have taken both tests. Write a one-page interpretation of the GGAT results. Use the T scores to compare the person's performance on the GGAT and on the IGAT. Use appropriate information from the Universal Demographic Sheet as part of the data for your interpretation.

QUESTIONS

1.   How well do the IGAT and the GGAT correlate (see *Step 10*)? What does this tell you about the tests?

2.   After reviewing the participants' information on the Universal Demographic Sheets, were there any patterns related to performance on the GGAT (e.g., male and female differences)?

3.   What are there some of the similarities and differences between individual and group tests? Answer for both the administrator and the examinee. Look at both the administration and scoring procedures.

SCRIPT FOR ADMINISTRATION OF THE GGAT

Use the following script to administer the GGAT to three college students. If possible, assemble them all in a room with enough space to work independently.

Say the following to the group:

Thank you very much for agreeing to participate in this exercise today. There are no known risks to participating in this exercise; however, you may be concerned about how well you are doing. Remember, this is <u>not</u> a real test. Try to do your best but don't worry if you cannot answer all of the questions.

You have the right to terminate your participation at any time during this study if you feel at all uncomfortable about continuing. The test that you are about to take has items that resemble those on tests of general ability. The GGAT consists of 30 items and should take about 15 to 20 minutes for you to complete. Even though they don't mean anything, results will be kept completely confidential, and your score will not be associated with your name. Do you agree to participate in this study? If so, please read and sign the Informed Consent Form.

Continue speaking:

Please complete the next page of your packet. It asks for general demographic information.

[GIVE PARTICIPANTS TIME TO COMPLETE THE FORM]

Continue speaking:

Please TURN TO THE TEST. PLACE YOUR ANSWER ON THE LINE NEXT TO THE QUESTION. PLEASE work independently and do not share information with others in the room. The test is not timed but work as quickly as is comfortable for you. Answer each question even if you are not sure. There is no penalty for guessing.

When you have finished with the test, please remain quiet until the others have finished. Does anyone have any questions? You may begin now.

[WHEN EVERYONE HAS FINISHED, COLLECT THE TESTS AND CONDUCT THE FOLLOWING DEBRIEFING]

Thank you for participating in this exercise. If you like, you can ask me about any of the questions that you might be curious about. However, remember this exercise was not a valid test of your ability, so please don't worry about the questions that you missed. The test was intentionally constructed to contain some very obscure material. Actually, we are learning about the administration of group tests in my class, and this exercise was designed to give us first-hand experience with the process of group test administration and scoring. Once again, your score will only be used in class exercises and will not be associated with your name. Do you have any questions?

Group General Ability Test (GGAT)

Examinee ID#_____

This is a test of your general mental ability. Each problem is followed by several answers. Please circle the letter of the correct answer under each test item on the test sheet.

1. The nationality of Beethoven was:
    (a) English.   (b) French.   (c) German.   (d) Russian.

2. The composer of "An American in Paris" was:
    (a) Bernstein.   (b) Stokowsky.   (c) Gershwin.   (d)Kelly.

3. The author of the play on which "My Fair Lady" is based is:
    (a) Goldsmith.   (b) Shaw.   (c) Fitzgerald.   (d) Baldwin.

4. Which planet in our solar system is nearest to the sun?
    (a) Venus   (b) Pluto   (c) Mercury   (d) Mars

5. What is the first month of the year that has exactly 30 days?
    (a) September   (b) February   (c) April   (d) June

6. In Greek mythology, who holds the world on his shoulders?
    (a) Atlas   (b) Jupiter   (c) Zeus   (d) Prometheus

7. Which continent is really a large island?
    (a) Asia   (b) Australia   (c) Africa   (d) Antarctica

8. The heaviest (weight) president of the United States was:
    (a) T. Roosevelt.   (b) A. Johnson.   (c) Jefferson.   (d) Taft.

9. *A Tale of Two Cities* was written by:
    (a) Defoe.   (b) Sade.   (c) Dickens.   (d) Poe.

10. *The Great Gatsby* was written by:
    (a) Fitzgerald.   (b) Lewis.   (c) Hawthorne.   (d) James.

11. The author of *Soul on Ice* is:
    (a) Baldwin.   (b) Haley.   (c) Cleaver.   (d) Parks.

12. *Leaves of Grass* was written by:
    (a) Whittier.   (b) Sandburg.   (c) Whitman.   (d) Thoreau.

13. Decline is to Accept as Imperfect is to:
    (a) Deficient.   (b) Flawless.   (c) Defective.   (d) Scanty.

14. Good is to Quality as Much is to:
    (a) Goods.   (b) Income.   (c) Produce.   (d) Quantity.

15. Ear is to Hear as Eye is to:
    (a) Seek.   (b) See.   (c) Blink.   (d) Distance.

16. Singer is to Aria as Actor is to:
    (a) Scene.   (b) Script.   (c) Soliloquy.   (d) Dialogue.

17. The distance between the bases in baseball is_____ feet.
    (a) 75   (b) 90   (c) 100   (d) 150

18. Comprehend means the same as:
    (a) Understand.   (b) Describe.   (c) Determine.   (d) Construct.

19. Redundant means the same as:
    (a) Loud.   (b) Superfluous.   (c) Ignorant.   d) Devious.

20. A "hog" is a term used to describe a form of:
    (a) car.   (b) bus.   (c) taxi.   (d) motorcycle.

21. Epistle means the same as:
    (a) Saint.   (b) Letter.   (c) Plant.   (d) Religion.

22. Salacious means the same as:
    (a) Tenacious.   (b) Salty.   (c) Lustful.   (d) Significant.

23. APRSOV
    How many of the following sets of letters are exactly like the above example?
        APRSVO   ARPSVO   APRSOV
            APRSOV   ASPRVO   ARSPOV

    (a) One   (b) Two   (c) Three   (d) Four

24. LBKMRSVO
    How many of the following sets of letters are exactly like the above example?
        LBKMRSVO   LKBRMSVO   LBKMSRVO
          LBKRMSVO   LBKMVSOR   LBMKRSVO

    (a) One   (b) Two   (c) Three   (d) Four

25. Which of the following numbers belongs with these numbers: 5, 7, 10, 14?
    (a) 18   (b) 16   (c) 19   (d) 20

26. Which of the following numbers completes the series: 4, 12, 6, 18?
    (a) 8   (b) 9   (c) 36   (d) 10

27. Pretend you fold a square piece of paper once on the diagonal. Fold it again so it forms a triangle, and then punch a hole through the triangle. If you unfold the sheet, how many holes are in it?
    (a) 1   (b) 2   (c) 4   (d) 8

28. Based on his average, a data clerk can input a record in 1.5 minutes. How many records can he input in 1 hour?
    (a) 45   (b) 30   (c) 40   (d) 60

29. If the first four pieces were put together, which Figure would they look like?

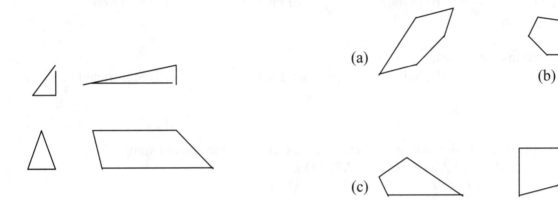

(a)

(b)

(c)

(d)

30. If the first figure were made into a three-dimensional figure, which Figure would it look like?

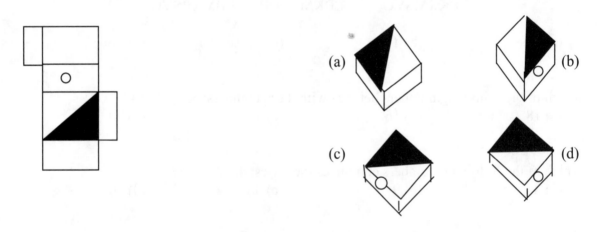

(a)

(b)

(c)

(d)

TOTAL # RIGHT: _____

GGAT ANSWER KEY

PAGE 1	PAGE 2	PAGE 3	PAGE 4
1. C	10. A	21. B	29. C
2. C	11. C	22. C	30. C
3. B	12. C	23. B	
4. C	13. B	24. A	
5. C	14. D	25. C	
6. A	15. B	26. B	
7. B	16. C	27. C	
8. D	17. B	28. C	
9. C	18. A		
	19. B		
	20. D		

GGAT SUMMARY DATA SHEET

Place the Total Right scores for those individuals who have also taken the IGAT in the column for Examinee #3. **Note:** Examiner = class member.

	Examinee #1	Examinee #2	Examinee #3
Examiner # 1			
Examiner # 2			
Examiner # 3			
Examiner # 4			
Examiner # 5			
Examiner # 6			
Examiner # 7			
Examiner # 8			
Examiner # 9			
Examiner #10			
Examiner #11			
Examiner #12			
Examiner #13			
Examiner #14			
Examiner #15			
Examiner #16			
Examiner #17			
Examiner #18			
Examiner #19			
Examiner #20			

GGAT NORMS TABLE

RAW SCORE	Z SCORE	T SCORE	%ILE RANK	RAW SCORE	Z SCORE	T SCORE	%ILE RANK
1				16			
2				17			
3				18			
4				19			
5				20			
6				21			
7				22			
8				23			
9				24			
10				25			
11				26			
12				27			
13				28			
14				29			
15				30			

EXERCISE 5
ADMINISTERING AND SCORING A
PROJECTIVE PERSONALITY TEST (PPT)

INTRODUCTION

Projective tests typically consist of ambiguous stimulus materials that are presented to the participant. Participants are asked to use their imaginations to describe what the materials suggest or to tell a story about them. They must project meaning onto the test materials. The kind of story told or the kind of description given is then used to evaluate personality characteristics or needs and drives.

The Projective Personality Test (PPT) used in this exercise is <u>not</u> a real test. A real projective test would be much longer, and the interpretation of responses is much more complicated. This exercise consists of two inkblots and is similar to the Rorschach test in the steps involved in administration and scoring. Although the procedures used here parallel those used in the Rorschach test, there is absolutely no evidence that these items measure the same characteristics as do the original Rorschach items.

This exercise gives the student a chance to administer and score an imitation projective test. Although there is no evidence for the validity of any responses to this exercise, the experience of administering it does show how a projective test is given, and illustrates some of the challenges in scoring this type of material.

MATERIALS NEEDED

1	Copy of the Informed Consent Form Template (Appendix A)
2	Copies of the Universal Demographic Sheet (Appendix B)
1	Watch with a second hand
1	Fine tip red ballpoint pen
1	Fine tip blue ballpoint pen
2	# 2 sharp pencils
1	Pair of scissors
1	Bottle of paper glue
4	5X8 index cards or two sheets of heavy construction paper
2	Sets of 2 inkblots (use the pages provided as photocopying them will lose all the gray tones)
2	Clean manila folders
4	Copies of the two-sided PPT Recording Sheet (one of each inkblot for two examinees)
2	Copies of the PPT Behavioral Observations Sheet
1	Copy of the PPT Scoring Guidelines
2	Copies of the PPT Individual Scoring Sheet
1	Copy of the PPT Group Summary Sheet
1	Copy of the PPT Descriptive Statistics of Group Data sheet (each sheet holds data for eight class members)
1	Copy of the PPT Interpretive Guidelines

PROCEDURE

A.   ADMINISTRATION

        Step 1.   *Compose an Informed Consent Form.*
The class will create an informed consent form (Appendix A) to be given to all volunteer participants that will inform them of the nature and purpose of the exercise, and will reinforce the anonymity and confidentiality of any information requested.

        Step 2.   *Prepare materials.*
Each class member will put each inkblot on a 5X8 card (or a half-sheet piece of construction paper). This procedure will yield a total of four cards.
a.   Take the pages out of the manual.
b.   Trim the margins of each page so that they fit on 5X8 index cards.
c.   Mark the top of the back on each card with the word "TOP."

        Step 3.   *Review necessary information.*
Before recruiting participants,:
a.   review the PPT Behavioral Observations Sheet so that you know which behaviors and characteristics to pay attention to during the session.
b.   review the PPT Recording Sheet and the PPT Scoring Guidelines so that you will remember what to record.

        Step 4.   *Recruit participants.*
Each class member will recruit two participants and arrange to meet them one at a time in a quiet, distraction-free room.

        Step 5.   *Arrange testing situation.*
Before the participant arrives, arrange the testing room.
a.   Place two chairs at a 90° angle across an ample table space.
b.   Place the following on your side of the table:
      (1)   a stopwatch,
      (2)   red and blue pens,
      (3)   two inkblot cards (face down), and
      (4)   a manila folder containing:
            (a)   1 copy of the Informed Consent Form,
            (b)   2 copies of the PPT Recording Sheet,
            (c)   1 copy of the Universal Demographic Sheet (Appendix B), and
            (d)   1 copy of the PPT Behavioral Observations Sheet.

Step 6.   *Introduce the Free Association phase.*

Have your participant sit on the opposite side from your writing hand. Using your own words, give the participant the following information: ***I will be showing you two cards, one by one, that have designs made from inkblots. Look at each card I give you and tell me what you think it looks like or what it reminds you of. You may look at each card as long as you like, and be sure to tell me whatever you see on a card. When you have finished telling me what you see on the card, give it back to me so that I will know you are through with it.***

Steps 7 and 8 are performed simultaneously.

Step 7.   *Show the inkblots one at a time.*

    a.   Hand the first card to the participant with the inkblot facing up. Make sure the word "TOP" on the back is, in fact, at the top. Participants may turn the card any way they want but you should always give it to them in the top up position. If you see them starting to turn but hesitating, let them know it is OK to rotate the card. If participants ask questions, answer in a way that does not lead them in any way. Remember people may respond to all or part of the inkblot. They may respond with either what it reminds them of, or what it makes them think of. Tell them to tell you whatever comes to mind.

    b.   Using the second-hand on your watch, mark on the PPT Recording Sheet when they start looking at the 5X8 card and when they give it back. If participants are still responding after five minutes, gently move them on to the next card.

    c.   If participants say they cannot think of anything, encourage them to try. Be sure they have held it at least two minutes before letting them give up and go on to the next card.

    d.   If participants give two or more responses and indicate that they are finished, give them the next card. If participants have given only one response, encourage them to continue by saying for example: ***"Most people see more than one thing. Look at it a bit longer and tell me if anything else comes to mind."***

    e.   Repeat this procedure with each of the cards.

Step 8.   *Complete part of the PPT Recording Sheet.*

Use one PPT Recording Sheet for each inkblot. While the participant is looking at an inkblot, make note of the following items:

a.   Record the appropriate inkblot # (#1 or #2) at the top of the PPT Recording Sheet.

b.   For each card, record the time at which you give the card to the participant and, again, at the end of the responses. Put these times in the first column of the PPT Recording Sheet.

c.   In the "First Round Description of Response" (second) column, write down the essence of everything your participants say about what they see when looking at the card. Be careful not to interrupt them. You have to accurately record a participant's responses without influencing the person in any way. Write down specific things the person says. Do not rely on your memory. Later, in scoring, you will have to examine these responses in detail to determine the many different characteristics of each response. Attention to detail in recording will facilitate the scoring process.

Step 9.   *Introduce inquiry phase.*

a.   When both inkblots have been completed, ask examinee to move his/her chair so that he/she is facing in the same direction you are.

b.   Say: ***"Now I would like to ask you a few questions about your responses."***

c.   Give the participant a red and a blue pen.

Step 10.   *Make the inquiry.*

For each description of an inkblot, ask the following questions:

a.   ***Where in the inkblot is the _____ ?***

      (1)   Have the inkblot between you and the participant, and tell the participant to outline in red the part of the inkblot used for the response.

             Pay attention to whether a response is based on the whole inkblot, a large portion of it, a small detail in the inkblot, or the white space on the card.

      (2)   If another response utilizes some of the same area, have the participant use the blue pen to outline it.

b.   ***What about this reminded you of _____ ?***

In the "Answers to Inquiry Phase" (third) column of the PPT Recording Sheet, write down what the participant answers about what features of the inkblot the participant used for a particular response.

Step 11.   *Gather participant's information.*

    a.   After you have completed the inquiry, ask the participant to complete the Universal Demographic Sheet.

    b.   Thank your participant, and give him/her permission to leave.

    c.   Immediately after the participant leaves, complete the PPT Behavioral Observations Sheet.

B.   SCORING

Step 1.   *Complete the remainder of the PPT Recording Sheet.*

    a.   Review the PPT Scoring Guidelines again to become familiar with which behaviors and responses you are looking for.

    b.   You will now need to make some decisions about each response. Using the appropriate sections of the PPT Scoring Guidelines, make a decision about the following characteristics and record your decision on the PPT Recording Sheet:

        (1)   In the "LOC/PART" column, the letter or letter combination that describes the part of the inkblot circled by the participant in *Step 10*a.

        (2)   In the "DETERM" column, the letter or letter combination that corresponds to the answer given by the participant when asked what about the inkblot suggested that response (*Step 10*b).

        (3)   In the "CONTENT" column, the letter corresponding to the category of the response given by the participant.

Step 2.   *Complete the PPT Individual Scoring Sheet.*

This sheet takes into account responses from both inkblots for a given participant. Use the PPT Recording Sheets as the source of your data.

    a.   For the Total # of Responses, add the number of responses given to a single inkblot.

    b.   For the Average Time per Response:

        (1)   Subtract the beginning time from the ending time on a single inkblot.

        (2)   Divide by the total number of responses to that inkblot.

    c.   For the Location responses, add together all responses to both inkblots that used a particular location.

    d.   For the Determinants responses, add together all responses to both inkblots that used a particular reason for the response.

    e.   For the Content responses, add together all responses to both inkblots that fall into a particular category.

Step 3.   *Collate data.*
    a.   Combine the information from both of your participants' PPT
        Individual Scoring Sheets. Then, on the first line of the PPT
        Group Summary Sheet, record the following totals:
        (1)   total # of responses,
        (2)   average response time,
        (3)   total # of each Location response,
        (4)   total # of each Determinant response, and
        (5)   total # of each Content category.
    b.   Class members will share their data with the rest of the class, who
        will then complete their copies of the PPT Group Summary Sheet.

Step 4.   *Calculate descriptive statistics.*
The class will divide into four work groups. One group will assume
responsibility for items (1) and (2) from Step #3 in the Scoring section, the
other three groups will each take one of the other items (Location,
Determinants, and Content). For each item they will determine the
descriptive measures (mean, SD, median, and range). Some items are
recorded separately for each card and some are aggregated and, therefore,
are calculated for each type of response within that item (e.g., in Content,
calculate separately for H's, A's, O's, and L's). Using these numbers,
they will fill in the appropriate sections of the PPT Descriptive Statistics
of Group Data Sheet.

Step 5.   *Collate the data.*
Each group will share their results with the rest of the class, so that the rest
of the class may complete their PPT Descriptive Statistics of Group Data
Sheet.

C.   INTERPRETATION
Due to the fact that this is an exercise primarily in administration and scoring, your
interpretation will be limited to the few items for which you have guidelines. A real life
interpretation would involve many more variables and interpreting them in a much more
complex way. It would also be based on 8-10 inkblots, some of which have colors in
them, as well as shadings of black and gray. A real life interpretation would also involve
a comparison with norms from a much larger group of participants and accepted standard
interpretations of each variable.

Step 1.   *Compare individual results to group data.*
Using the PPT Group Summary Sheet as a reference, each student should
compare the data from each of their participants to the group results.

Step 2.   *Interpret individual results.*
Using the PPT Interpretive Guidelines, the comparison data from *Step 1* of this Interpretation section, the Universal Demographic Sheet, and the PPT Behavioral Observations Sheet as references, write a one-page interpretive report for each of your participants. **Note:** Remember that this interpretation is being based on non-standardized stimuli (i.e., the inkblots) and on only a few of the many variables that are normally used to create an actual interpretation. This is just to give you practice in the process.

QUESTIONS

1.   What parts of the administration did you find the easiest? Hardest?

2.   What parts of the scoring did you find the easiest? Hardest?

3.   Which parts of the scoring seemed to involve the most subjectivity? Which parts seemed to be more objective?

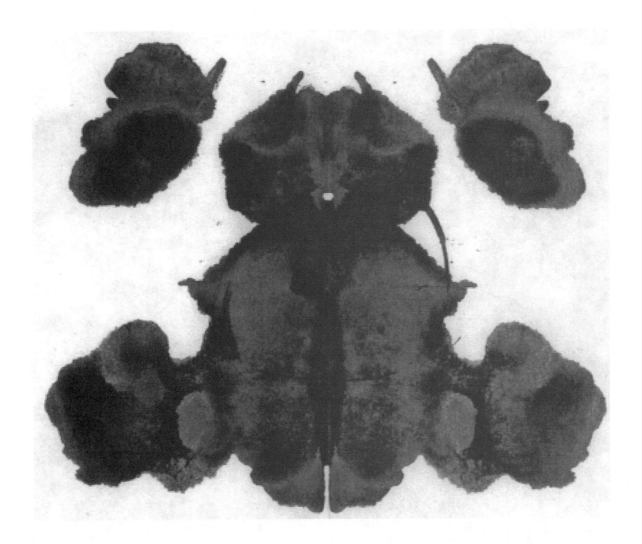

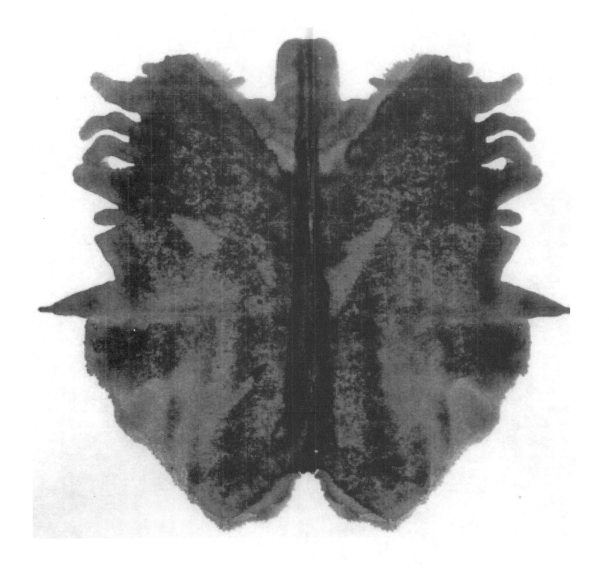

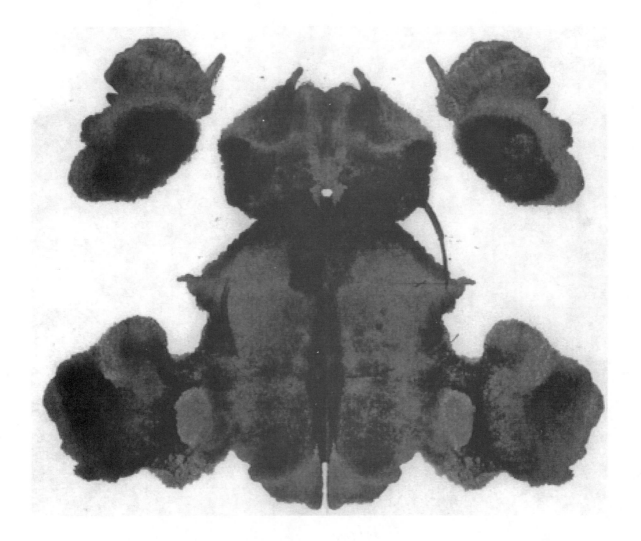

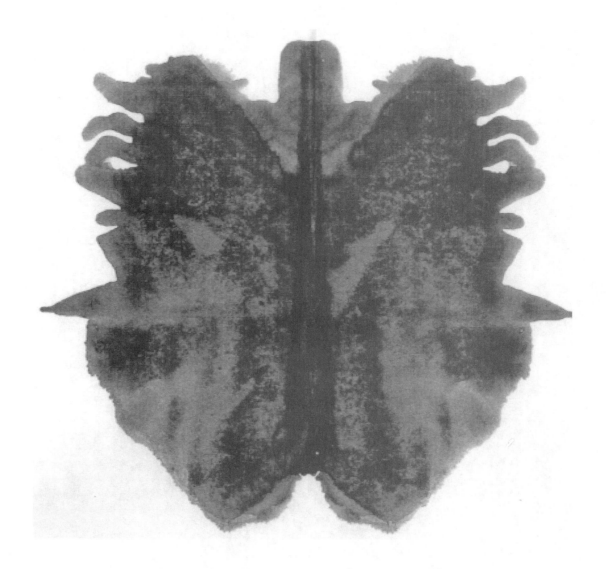

PPT RECORDING SHEET   INKBLOT # _____   Side #1

RESP. BEGIN / END	FIRST ROUND DESCRIPTION OF RESPONSE: Number each response. Use as many lines as needed for each response. Skip a line between responses.	ANSWERS TO INQUIRY PHASE	LOC/ PART	DE- TERM	CON- TENT

PPT RECORDING SHEET   INKBLOT #   Side #2

RESP. BEGIN / END	FIRST ROUND DESCRIPTION OF RESPONSE: Number each response. Use as many lines as needed for each response. Skip a line between each response.	ANSWERS TO INQUIRY PHASE	LOC./ PART	DE-TERM	CON-TENT

PPT BEHAVIORAL OBSERVATIONS SHEET

BEHAVIORS DURING TESTING

1. Appearance and posture (e.g., well-groomed, carries self with confidence, disorganized, disheveled):

    _____
    _____
    _____
    _____
    _____

2. Overall attitude toward this task (e.g., seemed slightly anxious, disinterested, bored, appeared to enjoy task):

    _____
    _____
    _____
    _____
    _____

3. Emotions displayed when looking at particular inkblots (e.g., inkblot #1 seemed to amuse, looked sad while reporting on inkblot #2):

    _____
    _____
    _____
    _____
    _____

4. Noteworthy remarks made by participant before or after testing (e.g., "I am nervous about this," "I feel I could have done more," "This was very hard for me to do"):

    _____
    _____
    _____
    _____
    _____

5. Level of satisfaction expressed about performance (e.g., "Maybe I'm not very creative," "I really think I did a good job"):

    _____
    _____
    _____
    _____
    _____

PPT SCORING GUIDELINES

Total # of Responses:

R = Total # of responses: Add up the number of responses given for both inkblots.

Average Time Per Response:

T/R = To calculate the average time it took to give a response, divide the total time the inkblot was held by the number of responses to that inkblot. You will calculate a T/R for each inkblot.

Location (Part of inkblot used from Administration Step 10a):

For each response, write the letter code corresponding to the part of the inkblot that the person indicates the place where they saw the response/object.

W	=	The whole blot is used.
D	=	A large section of the inkblot is used for the response (a part that is at least ¼ of the inkblot).
Dd	=	A small part of the inkblot or a very minor detail such as a single stray dot of ink.
S	=	White space

Determinants:

Write the letter code corresponding to the characteristic of the inkblot that prompted each response (from Administration *Step 10*b). A response can be scored with a combination of two codes. The dominant code is listed first.

F = Form: Form was the primary reason given for what reminded the participant of a particular response. Form answers will be distinguished in the following ways:

    F+: if the form is reasonable (e.g., on inkblot #1 a response of a "bug" based on the two "antennae" at the top the shape of the body).

    F-: if the form is not obviously related to the answer (e.g., the answer of "butterfly" to inkblot #1, with the reason being "the shape of it.").

T = Texture: The person bases his/her response on perceived texture (e.g., velvet, fluffy soft, gravelly, bumpy).

V = Vista: The person perceived a three dimensional or distant figure, citing shades of grey as the reason for of a particular response (e.g., looks like a picture taken from a plane where the mountains are darker).

Y = The person uses the shadings of gray, responding that the shadings themselves look like certain shapes (e.g., fuzzy cloth, clouds).

Content Categories:

For each response to an inkblot, choose the letter that indicates that the answer belongs in one of the following categories:

H	=	Human	A	=	Animal
O	=	Inanimate Object	L	=	Landscape or Sky View

PPT INDIVIDUAL SCORING SHEET

TOTAL # OF RESPONSES:

INKBLOT #1 ___   INKBLOT #2 _____

AVERAGE TIME PER RESPONSE (T/R):

INKBLOT #1 _____   INKBLOT #2 _____

TOTAL # OF RESPONSES GIVEN (from both inkblots) BASED ON LOCATION / PARTS OF INKBLOT:

W ___   D ___   Dd ___   S ___

TOTAL # OF RESPONSES (from both inkblots) BASED ON PARTICULAR DETERMINANTS:

F+ ___   F- ___   T ___   V ___   Y ____

TOTAL # OF RESPONSES (from both inkblots) CONTAINING A PARTICULAR CATEGORY OF CONTENT:

H ___   A ___   O ___   L ___

PPT GROUP SUMMARY SHEET
Page _____

ID #	Total # of Responses to an Inkblot		Avg. Time Per Response		Location Letters (both inkblots)				Determinants Used (both inkblots)					Content Categories (both inkblots)			
	#1	#2	#1	#2	W	D	Dd	S	F+	F-	T	V	Y	H	A	O	L

PPT DESCRIPTIVE STATISTICS OF GROUP DATA SHEET

A.   Number of Responses

INKBLOT 1

Total # of Responses _____   Mean # of Responses _____   S.D. _____

Median # of Responses _____   Modal # of Responses _____

INKBLOT 2

Total # of Responses _____   Mean # of Responses _____   S.D. _____

Median # of Responses _____   Modal # of Responses _____

B.   Average Time per Response

INKBLOT 1

Mean of the Means of Time/Response _____   S.D. _____

Median Average Response Time _____   Modal Average Response Time _____

INKBLOT 2

Mean of the Means of Time/Response _____   S.D. _____

Median Average Response Time _____   Modal Average Response Time _____

C.   Locations

Mean Frequency of "W" Response _____   S.D. _____

Median Frequency of "W" Response _____   Modal Frequency of "W" Response _____

Mean Frequency of "D" Response _____   S.D. _____

Median Frequency of "D" Response _____   Modal Frequency of "D" Response _____

Mean Frequency of "Dd" Response _____   S.D. _____

Median Frequency of "Dd" Response _____   Modal Frequency of "Dd" Response _____

Mean Frequency of "S" Response _____   S.D. _____

Median Frequency of "S" Response _____   Modal Frequency of "S" Response _____

D. Determinants

Mean Frequency of "F+" Response   _____   S.D. _____

Median Frequency of "F+" Response _____   Modal Frequency of "F+" Response_____

Mean Frequency of "F-" Response   _____   S.D. _____

Median Frequency of "F-" Response _____   Modal Frequency of "F-" Response_____

Mean Frequency of "T" Response   _____   S.D. _____

Median Frequency of "T" Response _____   Modal Frequency of "T" Response _____

Mean Frequency of "V" Response   _____   S.D. _____

Median Frequency of "V" Response _____   Modal Frequency of "V" Response _____

Mean Frequency of "Y" Response   _____   S.D. _____

Median Frequency of "Y" Response _____   Modal Frequency of "Y" Response _____

E. Content Categories

Mean Frequency of "H" Response   _____   S.D. _____

Median Frequency of "H" Response _____   Modal Frequency of "H" Response _____

Mean Frequency of "A" Response   _____   S.D. _____

Median Frequency of "A" Response _____   Modal Frequency of "A" Response _____

Mean Frequency of "O" Response   _____   S.D. _____

Median Frequency of "O" Response _____   Modal Frequency of "O" Response _____

Mean Frequency of "L" Response   _____   S.D. _____

Median Frequency of "L" Response _____   Modal Frequency of "L" Response _____

PPT INTERPRETIVE GUIDELINES

Remember that these guidelines are _very_ incomplete and simplistic. They are similar to ones used in testing but much more vague and limited. They are here only to show you what areas of functioning different aspects of the task refer to.

Number of responses:

Normally refers to level of intellectual activity. A low number of responses could imply depressive tendencies, defensiveness, or lower IQ. A high number could imply manic tendencies, obsessive traits or higher IQ.

Location (Part of inkblot used):

W =   Ability to organize their environment into meaningful wholes

D =   Ability to respond to obvious portions of their environment

Dd =   Could imply that a person is restricting their environment or obsessing. It is only interpreted if there are several responses using unusual details.

S =   Indicates contrariness or passive aggressive tendencies. It is only interpreted if there are several responses using the white space.

Determinants:

F =   The form of the inkblot is usually involved in 30-35% of responses. If there are a lot more than 35%, it can mean that the person is protecting self from showing emotion. If there are a lot less than 30%, it can mean that the person is experiencing some lack of order in his or her environment. A majority of F+ responses indicates that the person's perceptions are similar to the norm group.

T =   If the use of texture is high, it suggests a need for affection or closeness.

V =   If "vista" is used, it suggests that the person may be putting distance between self and outside world due to turning toward what is happening inside him- or herself. It is more common in adolescents than in adults.

Y =   If the "grayness" of the inkblot is used to respond to, this may be associated with situational stress. It can indicate possible feelings of helplessness or loss of control.

Content Categories:

H =   A total absence of this type of response can be associated with a lack of interest in others or with self-image problems.

A =   Animal responses usually occur in 35-45% of responses. If the number is much lower, it can be that the person may be over intellectualizing or too much value on being unique. If it is a lot more than 50% animal responses, the person may be defensive or is taking the easy way out in this task.

O / L = The interpretation of either inanimate objects or landscape views depends on the meaning of the particular item selected in normal usage (e.g., gun = aggression; flower = sensitivity).

EXERCISE 6
ADMINISTERING AND SCORING AN IN-BASKET TEST (IBT)

INTRODUCTION

In-basket tests are "simulations" that require a person to assume the role of a manager and to make decisions based on information supplied in a hypothetical "in" basket at work. Although they differ in approach from many other tests used in assessment, they are, nonetheless, tests in that they are samples of behavior used as part of an assessment in a particular situation. In this instance, the in-basket type of simulation is designed to help assess a person's cognitive and behavioral reactions to "real world" job-related tasks. Simulations often deal with such managerial duties as planning and organizing, decision-making, analyzing problems, or being sensitive to others' needs.

The development of in-basket simulations, therefore, should be based on a current job analysis and a current job description. These tests are timed for two reasons: (1) no decisions in the workplace are made without time limits, and (2) it is important to assess how well a person thinks and reacts under time pressure.

Simulation tasks result in various scores that give evidence of how well people deal with other people (fellow employees, customers, and/or supervisors), of the depth of their responses to problems posed, and of the amount of effort they put forth (i.e., number of items responded to in the allotted time). To keep this exercise to a reasonable length, it presents only a sample of items.

This exercise provides experience in administering and scoring an in-basket simulation to assess performance on a specified task. Each participant will be put in the role of a restaurant manager and will be given an in-basket packet containing memos, letters, flyers, a calendar, and other information that managers might encounter on a weekly basis. Participants will be judged only on the behavioral dimension of "Dealing with Employees" (an aspect of managerial performance).

MATERIALS NEEDED

1	Copy of the Informed Consent Form Template (Appendix A)
2	Copies of the Universal Demographic Sheet (Appendix B)
1	Stopwatch or a watch with a second hand
1	Red pen
2	Sharp #2 pencils
1	Pad of letter size lined paper
1	Envelope containing at least one dozen paper clips
2	Clean manila folders
2	Copies of the:
	IBT Exercise Instructions
	IBT Exercise (nine pages)
	IBT Feedback Form
	IBT Scoring Sheet
2	Copies of the Correlation Data Sheet and Computation (Appendix C)
1	Copy of the Computation of Student's *t* (Appendix D)

PROCEDURE

A.   ADMINISTRATION

Step 1.   *Compose an Informed Consent Form.*
The class will create an informed consent form (Appendix A) to be given to all volunteer participants that will inform them of the nature and purpose of the exercise, and will reinforce the anonymity and confidentiality of any information requested.

Step 2.   *Prepare materials.*

a.   In each of the two manila folders, place the following items in order from top to bottom:
(1)   Informed Consent Form,
(2)   Universal Demographic Sheet (Appendix B),
(3)   IBT Exercise Instructions, and
(4)   IBT Exercise.
Note: Each page of the in-basket packet has an item number in the lower, right-hand corner. Put these pages in the folder in *exact* order.

b.   Assign a random ID # to each participant, and place that same number on all documents for each participant on the Universal Demographic Sheet, on the IBT Exercise Instructions, on all exercise sheets, on the IBT Feedback Form, and on the IBT Scoring Sheet.

Step 3.   *Recruit participants.*
Each class member will test two undergraduate college students. If possible, one person should be a Business major and one person a non-Business major.

Step 4.   *Introduce task.*

a.   Test each person individually, in a quiet, relatively distraction-free room.

b.   Once the person is seated,:
(1)   introduce yourself and give a general explanation of the task.
(2)   give the participant the Informed Consent Form to sign. Once the consent form is signed and collected, give the participant a numbered Universal Demographic Sheet and ask him/her to complete it.
(3)   give the person next a prepared manila folder, a red pen, an envelope of paper clips, a pad of letter-sized lined paper, and two sharpened pencils.
(4)   ask the participant to open the folder and read the "IBT Exercise Instructions" page.
(5)   answer any questions the participant might have.

Step 5. *Administer the in-basket exercise.*

    a.   Ask the participant to arrange the pad of paper, the pen and the pencils, the paper clips and the manila folder in a way that is comfortable.

    b.   Instruct the participant to read each of the pages provided and respond or suggest action to be taken. This should be done in writing, either on the particular page or on the pad. If writing on a separate page of paper, paperclip the response page to the appropriate In-Basket item.

    c.   Tell the participant you will return in 20 minutes.

    d.   Ask the participant to turn to the IBT exercise and begin.

Step 6. *Collect responses.*
Return in 20 minutes and collect the in-basket exercise.

Step 7. *Obtain feedback.*
Give the participant a numbered IBT Feedback Form. Ask the person to use the scale provided to rate how well he/she did on the task.

B.   SCORING AND ANALYSIS

Step 1. *Score exercise.*
Assess each participant's performance on the task using the IBT Scoring Sheet.

Step 2. *Record data.*
Each class member shall record the scores of the participants they tested and the participants' own evaluation scores on the first line of the appropriate Correlation Data Sheet (Appendix C). One sheet is used for Business majors and one sheet is used for non-Business majors.

Step 3. *Combine class data.*
Class members will share their data with the rest of the class so that all will have completed Correlation Data Sheets.

Step 4. *Correlate objective and subjective scores.*
Once all the performance scores for the class have been collected, compute the correlation (Appendix C) between the self-evaluation scores and the actual performance scores. Do this separately for the Business majors and for the non-Business majors.

Step 5.   *Investigate possible differences between groups.*

a.   Using the data from the "Business and "non-Business" majors, each class member will compute an independent group's *t* test (Appendix D) to investigate the significance of the difference between the IBT scores.

b.   Using a Table of Significance for *t*, class members will determine the *p* value of the obtained *t* value (area in tail).

QUESTIONS

1.   How well did the person's self-rating of task performance correlate with the actual task scores? If there is a low correspondence, why would there be?

2.   What were the results of the comparison of the mean scores between the Business and non-Business majors? What did you expect the results to be? Were your expectations supported?

3.   Based on your readings and what you learned through doing this exercise, how effective is this assessment approach? Explain your answer and integrate with class readings.

IBT EXERCISE INSTRUCTIONS

You are Chris Morgan, manager of a Western States Restaurant.

Today is Saturday, April 17 at 11:30 a.m. You are currently in the middle of a weeklong out-of-town trip, part convention and part vacation. You left Wednesday, April 14. The convention is Saturday through Tuesday (April 17-20), but you extended your time off to a full week in order to take a brief vacation before the convention activities. You expect to return next Wednesday morning (April 21).

Back in Western City, your recently appointed Assistant Manager Pat Sharpe is running the restaurant in your absence. At approximately 10:00 a.m. today you received an Overnight Express package from Pat Sharpe. This package contains materials that have accumulated in your in-basket over the past few days, including a few things that you had not responded to before you left.

Included in the package is a memo indicating that Pat Sharpe is keeping busy with the day-to-day running of the restaurant and thought you had better handle these items. Because Pat was promoted to assistant manager not long ago, she does not feel comfortable handling your correspondence and you do not feel comfortable having her take care of such things at this time unless you give specific instructions.

You have conference activities planned for the duration of this afternoon, including a presentation you're scheduled to make at 12:00 noon. Due to the fact that many of these items need immediate attention, you need to respond promptly to the materials you received and get them mailed out to the restaurant this afternoon. With the presentation being at noon, you have only 20 minutes to respond to the in-basket materials and still have enough time to get to the meeting room.

Your responses should be written in the form of letters, memos, instructions, etc. You may write directly on the items or on a separate page. Some of the material is simply informational (e.g., Wait Staff Work Schedule for April). If you wish to forward or delegate an item, you need to indicate who will get it and provide instructions either on the item or a separate memo. All materials will be sent Overnight Express to the restaurant and will be dealt with according to your instructions.

In summary:
- ✓ Today is Saturday, April 17 at 11:30 a.m. You left on Wednesday, April 14, and are returning Wednesday, April 21.
- ✓ You just received a package of things that have accumulated in your in-basket over the past few days. They need <u>immediate responses,</u> and <u>only you</u> can respond to them.
- ✓ You have only 20 minutes to respond to your in-basket materials.

DO NOT TURN PAGE UNTIL INSTRUCTED TO DO SO!

IBT EXERCISE

WESTERN STATES

DATE: 4/16

TO: Chris

FROM: Pat

RE: Important Information

CC:

I hope your vacation went fine! Here's some letters and memos I thought you should deal with. Good luck with your presentation. See you Wednesday. The whole staff is looking forward to the meeting to get new directions from you. Oh, I noticed a conflict in the schedule. You will not be back in time to meet with Chen Li at 2pm until Wednesday 4/21 but that meeting conflicts with the staff meeting at the same time. Do you want to notify Li or the staff of a meeting time change?

Item # 1A

APRIL

Sunday	Monday	Tuesday	Wednesday	Thursday	Friday	Saturday
				1	2	3
4	5 FAX Monthly Report to HQ	6 Doctor's appt, 9 am	7	8	9	10
11 Easter	12	13	14 Leave 7:20 AM, Flight #120 Vacation!	15 --------	16 ----------]	17 COMSTAD CONVENTION 12:00- Presentation
18	19 Meet Chen Li at my restaurant, 2pm (M-W this week)	20	21 Return 8:00 AM Flight #143 2:00-Staff Meeting	22	23 Mary's recital, 6 pm	24
25 Murphy lunch, 11am to 2 pm	26	27 Meet with Regional manager, 4 pm	28	29	30 Post May's work schedule Do inventory	

Item # 1B

WORK SCHEDULE, APRIL
WAIT STAFF

DATE: 3/27

COMPLETED BY: Chris Morgan

NAME	DAYS	STATION	SHIFT
Adrian Henle	Th,F,S,Sun T	6 6	6PM-2AM 1 PM-9PM
Todd Yen	Th,F,S,Sun W	5	8PM-2PM 10AM-3PM
Sam Pratt	F,S T,W,Th	4 2	8PM-2AM 5AM-10AM
Laura Sedillo	F,S,Sun Th	3 6	8PM-2AM 8PM-2AM
Miguel Ramirez	M,T,W,Th F	4 4	8PM-2AM 10AM-3PM
Dolores Darrock	W,Th,F,S Sun	1 1	8PM-2AM 10AM-3PM
Richard Jimenez	M,T,Sun Th,F	1 5	8PM-2AM 5AM-10AM
Chris Cooper	M,T,W,Th F	2 2	8PM-2AM 3PM-8PM
Ken Murphy	F,S,Sun T,W	2 3	8PM-2AM 5AM-10AM
Greg Garcia	M,T,W,Th F	3 2	8PM-2AM 3PM-8PM
Francine Smith	T,W Th,F	1 1	3PM-8PM 5AM-10AM
Kelly Mathews	T,W Th,F	2 2	3PM-8PM 5AM-10AM
Camille Rodgers	M,W,Th T,F	5 6	5AM-10AM 10AM-3PM
Chen Li	W,Th,S F	4 1	5AM-10AM 5AM-10AM
Jose Rodriguez	M,T,Th,F W	2 6	3PM-8PM 3PM-8PM

Item # 2

DATE: April 14

TO: Chris Morgan

FROM: Nicole Davalos

RE: Terry

CC:

Someone told me last night that she saw Terry Johnson leaving with a bottle of good wine from the restaurant. I recall seeing some suspicious activities like this a couple of weeks ago. Do you remember me mentioning this? How do you want me to handle this?

Item # 3

DATE: April 16
TO: Chris Morgan
FROM: Jackie Lee
RE: Dale
CC:

Dale was late this week several times. I warned him not to do it again but he keeps coming in late. I'm sick of having to cover for him. Next time he's late I'm going to fire him.

Item # 4

DATE:	April 16
TO:	Chris
FROM:	Nicole
RE:	Time off
CC:	

I was wondering if I could get Memorial Day weekend off? As you know, going up to the cabin is sort of a Memorial Day tradition for my family. You know how much fun the cabin is because both of our families have spent so much time together there. We should plan on spending the Fourth of July holiday with our families there again this year! I know it's policy to work every other holiday, but could you make an exception just this once? I probably wouldn't be asking if we weren't such good friends. Leave me a note as soon as you can because my husband needs to know immediately so he can get time off also. Please let me know by Monday.

Item # 5

DATE: April 13
TO: Chris
FROM: Adrian
RE: Promotion?
CC:

I want to set up a meeting with you ASAP! I have been here a long time (remember we started together!) and I don't feel that I have been treated fairly. Of the four of us that started together as waiters, I am the only one who has not advanced beyond headwaiter. I can't even remember the last time I got a raise! Further, I hear that you are going to recommend Nicole for the next promotion, when *I* should be next. Maybe if I was as good of friends with you as Nicole is, I wouldn't be in this situation. This sure isn't how the restaurant was described when I (we) was hired!

Item # 6

State Manager's Office

DATE: April 15
TO: Chris
FROM: John Markley, State Manager
RE: Unit Results
CC:

I am concerned about the quarterly figures and the trends shown in your restaurant. The financials cause concern, and the evidence shows declining customer satisfaction.

Please inform me of the action steps you plan to take to turn things around.

Item # 7

IBT FEEDBACK FORM

ID #: _____

On the following scale, rate how well you think you did on this in-basket exercise.

Circle the number that comes closest to your opinion of your performance.

1	2	3	4	5
Very Poor	Poor	Average	Good	Very Good

Please explain self-rating:_____
_____
_____
_____
_____
_____

IBT SCORING SHEET

ID #: _____   RATER: _____

DATE: _____/_____/_____   FINAL TOTAL RATING: _____

INSTRUCTIONS FOR SCORING:

On this form, place a check (√) in front of those behaviors demonstrated in the participant's response (or lack thereof) to the items listed. The number(s) in parentheses after each behavior refer(s) to the relevant document in the in-basket material. The (+) or (-) before a behavior item indicates a positive or negative value placed on the occurrence of the behavior.

In the comments section, write your own observations based on reviewing the in-basket exercise as a whole.

Dimension: "Dealing with Employees"   # of +'s _____   # of -'s _____

Treats People Fairly

_____ + Highlights disciplinary policy to Jackie Lee (#4)

_____ + Responds fairly to Terry about Nicole's memo (#3)

_____ + Turns down Nicole's request or tells Nicole she can only have the day off if she can switch shifts with another server (#5)

_____ + Tells Adrian that performance needs to improve (#6)

_____ + Tells Nicole not to accuse Terry or to jump to conclusions prematurely (#3)

_____ - Gives Nicole Memorial Weekend off automatically (#5)

_____ - Gives promotion to Adrian (#6)

_____ - Assumes wine was stolen by employee (#3)

_____ - Takes punitive action against Terry Johnson (#3)

Treats Employees with Respect

_____ + Tells Nicole why she does not receive time off (#5)

_____ - Fails to respond to wine problem (#3)

_____ - Talks down to any employee (various)

Acts Responsibly with Respect to Others

_____ + Accurately paraphrases information in return memos (#1A, #3 through #7)

_____ + Responds to the concerns of John Markley, State Manager about the financial trends of the restaurant (#7)

_____ - Fails to notify Chen Li that will have to miss the meeting (#1B)

Comments: _____

_____

_____

_____

_____

_____

_____

_____

OVERALL SCORING

Subtract the number of Minus (-) items checked from the number of Plus (+) items checked.

Using the guide below, rate the participant's overall performance on the test dimension "Dealing with Employees" (1 = Very Low to 5 = Very High).

If the total difference obtained between Pluses and Minuses is:
-7 to -5, Final Total Rating = 1
-4 to -1, Final Total Rating = 2
 0 to +2, Final Total Rating = 3
+3 to +5, Final Total Rating = 4
+6 to +8, Final Total Rating = 5

Note: The verbal equivalents of these Final Total Ratings are:

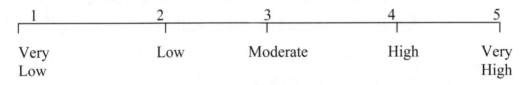

1	2	3	4	5
Very Low	Low	Moderate	High	Very High

Place this **Final Total Rating** (# and verbal equivalent) at the top of first page on this IBT Scoring Sheet.

EXERCISE 7
OBSERVATION AND ASSESSMENT OF BEHAVIOR IN THE FIELD (FOA)

INTRODUCTION
In many areas in the research and practice of psychology, it is advantageous to make observations and assessments of behavior in naturalistic settings. For example, a child psychologist may observe aggressive behavior among children during a recreational activity. An industrial psychologist may observe work behavior on the job and make ratings of employee performance. In both of these situations, the psychologist is conducting a field observation and an assessment of behavior.

The purpose of this exercise is to give students practice in the following two sequential steps in behavioral observation: (1) observe and record behaviors, and then (2) rate effectiveness of performance. The first part takes students through the various steps of building a behavioral observation rating tool, including the identification of relevant performance dimensions and the specification of exemplar behaviors that reflect performance on those dimensions. In the second part of the exercise, students use these behavioral observations to make final ratings on the performance dimensions with behaviorally anchored rating scales (BARS). A behaviorally based scale is one in which behavioral statements "anchor" the numerical levels of a scale. These behaviors provide benchmarks against which to compare observed behavior when determining a rating. The steps in this exercise can be applied to any naturalistic setting. In this exercise, "customer service quality" was chosen as the target due to the many opportunities students have to observe the relevant behaviors.

MATERIALS NEEDED
1	Copy of the Dimensions of Customer Service Quality
1	Copy of the Tips for Observation of Behavior in the Field
1	Copy of the Tips for Assessment of Behavior in the Field
2	Copies of the Behavior Observation Sheet
2	Copies of the Customer Service Quality Behaviorally Anchored Rating Scales

PROCEDURE
A. SPECIFICATION AND OBSERVATION OF RELEVANT BEHAVIORS

Step 1. *Choose observational targets.*

The purpose of this field observation assessment is to observe and rate dimensions of customer service quality. Individuals (or groups) must first decide what customer service occupational setting they would like to use for the assessment.

a. The setting should allow each student to interact with a customer service representative for an extended period of time in order to make a complete assessment of customer service quality. Examples of appropriate settings include:

(1) Food service (e.g., a restaurant server; not a fast food cashier)

(2) Retail customer service representative (e.g., sales person for an automobile, appliance, or electronics)

          (3)   Phone or in-person customer support (e.g., technical support)

          (4)   Personal banker

          (5)   Fitness trainer

b.   When choosing an occupation to observe, remember that you will be making detailed assessments of customer service quality. Choose an occupation setting where you are interacting with an employee for at least several minutes. **Note:** A cashier would not give you the opportunity to make a detailed behavioral assessment.

c.   After you have chosen an occupation, write down the position name and company where you will be making the observation on each of the Customer Service Quality Behaviorally Anchored Rating Scales. Each student will rate two individuals in the occupation selected.

Step 2.   *Review customer service quality dimensions.*
Each student (or group) should then review the Dimensions of Customer Service Quality. Each of the six dimensions reflects a different aspect of customer service quality and will be a targeted competency that will be observed in this field study.

To understand how the dimensions are different from each other, the class should discuss how a customer service person in a given job could be effective in one dimension and not effective in the second. For example, is it possible for the employee to be:

a.   Responsive yet not Competent?

b.   Effective in Communication but not at all Timely?

Step 3.   *Generate list of critical behaviors of interest.*
After reviewing each of the customer service quality dimensions, each individual (or group) will then generate a list of critical behaviors that reflect the dimension of interest. For each dimension:

a.   Review the definition for the dimension.

b.   Brainstorm example behaviors that reflect both effective and ineffective performance on that dimension *for the position you have chosen to observe.* For example, an effective behavior for a travel agent on "Timeliness" might be "completed transaction in expected time frame" while an example of an ineffective behavior for "Competence" might be "did not know how to book the ticket."

c.   Using Part A, B, and C of the Behavioral Observation Sheet, write three to five of these behaviors for each dimension in the "Critical Behavior of Interest" column. Please keep in mind that these behaviors should be tailored for the position you will be observing and these will be the behaviors you will be looking for during your assessment.

Step 4.   *Review Tips for Observation of Behavior in the Field.*
Before conducting your field observation, review the Tips for Observation of Behavior in the Field. This form lists some helpful information to keep in mind and some observational errors to avoid when conducting your field observation.

Step 5.   *Conduct the behavior observation.*
a.   To be fair to each employee, observe each one separately (i.e., do not observe two customer service employees at the same time). Observe each employee in his or her natural work setting.
b.   As you observe each employee's behavior, it is critical that you take detailed and thorough notes using the Behavioral Observation Sheet with the list of critical behaviors that you created. This will allow you to justify your decisions when making your final ratings on each of the dimensions.
    (1)   If you observe a critical behavior of interest from the employee for a certain dimension, place a check ($\sqrt{}$) in the corresponding box on your Behavioral Observation Sheet.
    (2)   During the observation, make additional notes of other relevant, specific behaviors for each dimension on the "Other relevant behaviors observed" section of the Behavioral Observation Sheet.
c.   If you are unable to take notes during the actual behavioral observation (e.g., you are observing your interaction with the employee), complete the Behavioral Observation Sheet immediately after the observation to ensure accuracy.

B.   ASSESSMENT OF PERFORMANCE EFFECTIVENESS
Step 1.   *Review Tips for Assessment of Behavior in the Field.*
Before rating each employee on the relevant dimensions, review the Tips for Assessment of Behavior in the Field. This form lists some helpful information to keep in mind and some rating errors to avoid when making your final ratings for each dimension.

Step 2.   *Review behavioral observations.*
When making a rating for each dimension of customer service quality, review your notes from the Behavior Observation Sheet. Identify which of the critical behaviors you observed from the employee and review the additional "Other relevant behaviors observed" for each employee.

Step 3.   *Make final rating on each of the dimensions.*
For each employee you observed, make a final rating on each of the dimensions using the Customer Service Quality Behaviorally Anchored Rating Scales.
a.   Read the behavioral anchors for each level of the scale when making your final rating decision. Compare the behavior you

observed to the example behaviors. It is important to note that the behaviors listed on the rating scale are only examples, and that the employees you observed are likely to demonstrate a range of behaviors that are different from the anchors. Rate the participant's actual behavior instead of forcing the behaviors to match the examples.

b. The scale represents a five-point continuum of proficiency on the dimension from 1 (*needs improvement*) to 5 (*highly proficient*). A good way to think about the rating points is as follows:

5: The behaviors exhibited by the employee clearly exceed the dimension definition. The employee exhibits behaviors that exemplify go "above and beyond" that which is specified.

3: The behaviors exhibited by the employee clearly meet the standards set forth by the dimension definition.

1: The behaviors exhibited by the employee clearly do not meet the standards set forth by the dimension definition.

c. Make your final rating for each dimension by circling the number on the scale that represents each employee's performance on the rating.

QUESTIONS

1. Which dimensions were the most difficult for you to observe relevant behaviors?

2. After your observation, were there other behaviors you observed that you had not considered for each of your dimensions? If so, what were they?

3. What are your final ratings on each of the customer service dimensions for each employee? What would you conclude about their overall customer service quality?

DIMENSIONS OF CUSTOMER SERVICE QUALITY

1. **Meeting customer needs**
   Definition: gathers relevant, complete, and accurate information to identify customer needs; provides clear and accurate solution for customer.

   Example behaviors: _____

2. **Competence**
   Definition: employee possesses the knowledge, skills, and/or abilities to perform and provide customer service.

   Example behaviors: _____

3. **Responsiveness**
   Definition: employee is ready and willing to provide service; employee is accessible and approachable to customer; employee responds directly and fully to customer questions or suggestions.

   Example behaviors: _____

4. **Timeliness**
   Definition: responds to customers in a timely manner; adheres to time frame expectations for delivery of customer service.

   Example behaviors: _____

5. **Effective communication**
   Definition: asks questions and conveys information to customer in a clear, unambiguous, and effective way; actively listens; communicates at an appropriate technical level that the customer can understand.

   Example behaviors: _____

6. **Customer value**
   Definition: employee is courteous, respectful, considerate, and empathetic; employee has the customer's best interests at heart.

   Example behaviors: _____

TIPS FOR OBSERVATION OF BEHAVIOR IN THE FIELD

1. During the assessment, carefully observe as many specific details as you can; attend carefully to what is said and done.

2. Write down only specific behaviors related to each of your dimensions; avoid general impressions. Pay attention to both verbal behavior and nonverbal behavior (e.g., tone of voice and eye contact).

3. Take complete notes on the employee you are observing; write down as much as you can about the person you are rating. Avoid abbreviation and simplification of information.

4. Consider behaviors throughout the observation, not just those at the beginning (primacy effect) or end (recency effect) of the observation.

5. Avoid making quick decisions early on during the observation. This will lead you to spend the remaining time searching for a justification of this decision. Instead take detailed notes throughout the observation and evaluate the responses only after the observation is over.

TIPS FOR ASSESSMENT OF BEHAVIOR IN THE FIELD

1. Avoid the "halo" error. Halo refers to an instance when an observation of one dimension (or a global impression) influences perceptions of behaviors on other dimensions. For example, halo occurs when an assessor rates an employee high on effective communication simply because he or she is also high on customer value. To avoid halo, separate the various dimensions you are observing in your mind and make separate observations for each behavioral dimension. *Keep in mind that each attribute is unique*; remember that a person can by highly effective in one dimension yet need improvement on a different dimension.

2. When rating multiple individuals, do not let ratings of one person influence ratings of another person.

3. Beware of stereotyping. Remember that you are rating the employee based on performance during the observation. You should not consider his or her group membership (e.g., race, gender, or age) when making your final rating decisions.

4. Do not let one aspect of an employee's performance or response overshadow another aspect. Instead, place equal importance on all of the employee's behavior when making your rating decision rather than concentrating on one particular response.

BEHAVIORAL OBSERVATION SHEET, PART A

Dimension 1: Meeting Customer Needs

Critical Behavior of Interest	Observed ? (√)
1.	
2.	
3.	
4.	
5.	

Other relevant behaviors observed: _____

_____

_____

Dimension 2: Competence

Critical Behavior of Interest	Observed ? (√)
1.	
2.	
3.	
4.	
5.	

Other relevant behaviors observed: _____

_____

_____

BEHAVIORAL OBSERVATION SHEET, PART B

Dimension 3: Responsiveness

Critical Behavior of Interest	Observed ? (√)
1.	
2.	
3.	
4.	
5.	

Other relevant behaviors observed: _____

_____

_____

Dimension 4: Timeliness

Critical Behavior of Interest	Observed ? (√)
1.	
2.	
3.	
4.	
5.	

Other relevant behaviors observed: _____

_____

_____

BEHAVIORAL OBSERVATION SHEET, PART C

Dimension 5: Effective Communication

Critical Behavior of Interest	Observed ? (√)
1.	
2.	
3.	
4.	
5.	

Other relevant behaviors observed: _____

_____

_____

Dimension 6: Customer Value

Critical Behavior of Interest	Observed ? (√)
1.	
2.	
3.	
4.	
5.	

Other relevant behaviors observed: _____

_____

_____

CUSTOMER SERVICE QUALITY
BEHAVIORALLY ANCHORED RATING SCALES

Observation Date: ____ / ____ / _____   Duration of Observation: _____

Position: _____   Company: _____

Meeting Customer Needs

1	2	3	4	5
Failed to identify customer need and did not provide appropriate solution.		Partially identified customer need and adequately addressed customer issue.		Correctly identified customer issue and provided appropriate solution.

Competence

1	2	3	4	5
Lacked the knowledge, skills, and/or ability to provide customer service.		Had adequate levels of the knowledge, skills, and/or abilities needed.		Had superior levels of the knowledge, skills, and/or ability needed.

Responsiveness

1	2	3	4	5
Employee was not accessible or approachable.		Employee was approachable but was not easily accessible.		Employee was approachable and willing to provide service.

Timeliness

1	2	3	4	5
Did not respond in expected time frame.		Responded slowly or longer than expected.		Responded to customer in a timely manner.

Effective Communication

1	2	3	4	5
Communicated using unfamiliar and vague language.		Spoke clearly but occasionally used slang or made mistakes.		Actively listened; communicated clearly, effectively, and appropriately.

Customer Value

1	2	3	4	5
Lacked respect and consideration in interaction with customer.		Was courteous but fails to empathize with customer.		Was courteous, respectful, and empathetic with the customer.

EXERCISE 8
ADMINISTERING AND SCORING A PHYSICAL ABILITY TEST (PHT)

INTRODUCTION

Physical abilities are important for successful performance in a number of jobs, ranging from the fine finger dexterity needed for jobs such as dental assistant and seamstress to the strength needed for fire fighters and heavy construction. Testing for these physical abilities is an important ingredient in vocational counseling, employment referrals, and personnel selection.

Physical ability tests can be compared to other psychological tests in terms of their "stimuli" and required "overt" responses. On one hand, the majority of traditional "paper-and-pencil" psychological tests measuring constructs such as aptitude or attitudes require an examinee to read a question or statement on a piece of paper and then respond to the item by making a simple mark. The stimulus in this testing situation is the printed words or numbers on the paper, and the overt response is the required mark the examinee makes on a piece of paper.

Physical ability tests, on the other hand, involve much more complex stimuli and overt responses. In one physical ability test, for example, the stimulus may be a pegboard, and the overt response made by the examinee is to place small pieces of metal in the open holes. Another example of a modern physical ability test is a speed and accuracy computer typing test. The rationale for the development and use of physical ability tests is to measure concrete human abilities (e.g., eye-hand coordination, strength, reaction time) that are important for successful job performance.

The purpose of this exercise is to give students experience administering and taking different types of physical ability tests and to recognize the types of psychological and physical abilities that can be measured by these tests. Although physical ability tests can include the use of a complex apparatus (e.g., Purdue Pegboard, Minnesota Rate of Manipulation Test, Pursuit Rotor, O'Connor Tweezer Dexterity Test), the ability tests in this exercise mimic paper-and-pencil tests such as those found in the MacQuarrie Test of Mechanical Aptitude.

MATERIALS NEEDED

2	Sharpened pencils
1	Stopwatch or wristwatch with a second hand
1	Large plastic cup
10	Pennies
10	Nickels
10	Dimes
10	Large paperclips
10	Small paperclips
3	Copies of the PHT Tracing Test
3	Copies of the PHT Dotting Test
3	Copies of the PHT Pursuit Test
1	Copy of the PHT Scoring Sheet

PROCEDURE

Step 1.   *Read background information.*

Before beginning the exercise, it is important to understand specific dimensions of physical ability assessment and related testable aspects of performance. Each class member should become familiar with one or both of the following information sources that explain lists of physical abilities that are both the basis of physical ability testing and this exercise:

     a.   Fleishman, E. A. & Reilly, M. E. (1992). *Handbook of human abilities: Definitions, measurements, and job task requirements.* Palo Alto, CA: Consulting Psychologists Press.

     b.   O*NET Ability descriptions: *http://online.onetcenter.org/find/descriptor/browse/Abilities/*

Step 2.   *Assemble workgroups.*

For this exercise, students will be working in groups of three to administer the Physical Ability Test (PHT). Students will take turns so that each person in the group has the opportunity to administer and take each part of the PHT. Write the names of each group member (examinee) on the PHT Scoring Sheet.

Step 3.   *Administer the PHT Sorting Test.*

     a.   For the PHT Sorting Test, each group will need a stopwatch (or wristwatch with a second hand), a large plastic cup, 10 pennies, 10 nickels, 10 dimes, 10 large paperclips, and 10 small paperclips.

     b.   Before the test begins, the administrator should place all of the coins and paperclips in the plastic cup and thoroughly mix the objects together.

              To begin the test, the test administrator will read the following instructions <u>carefully</u>:

              This is the Sorting Test for the PHT. When I say "GO!" you will pour the contents of the cup onto the table and, using both hands, sort the items into five piles as quickly as you can. You will sort the pennies into one pile, the nickels in a second, the dimes in a third, the large paperclips in a fourth, and the small paperclips in a fifth pile. Ready, GO!

     c.   After announcing the start of the test, the administrator will start timing the examinee using the stopwatch. When the examinee has finished sorting the objects, immediately stop the stopwatch and record the time (in seconds) on the PHT Scoring Sheet (examinees should also record their own time on the PHT Scoring Sheet).

     d.   Group members will then switch roles until everyone has administered and taken the test.

Step 4.   *Administer the PHT Tracing Test.*

     a.   For the PHT Tracing Test, each group will need a watch, a sharpened pencil, and three copies of the test.

b.	To begin the test, the test administrator will read the following instructions <u>carefully</u>:
This is the Tracing Test for the PHT. Notice the little black triangle under the word "Start." When I say "GO!" you are to begin at the little triangle and draw a curved line with your pencil through the small openings in the horizontal lines without touching them. Draw down the grid first and then up in one continuous line. Be careful when drawing your line not to touch any of the horizontal lines as you will be penalized ½ second for each line you touch. Ready, GO!

c.	After announcing the start of the test, the administrator will start timing the examinee using the stopwatch. When the examinee has reached the end of the test, immediately stop the stopwatch and record the time (in seconds) on the bottom of the PHT Tracing Test.

d.	Next, the administrator will carefully examine the line drawn by the examinee. Circle any points where the line drawn touches any of the horizontal lines on the test. Note the number of these mistakes on the PHT Tracing Test.

e.	Multiply the number of mistakes by ½ and add this number to the tracing test time. Write this final time on the bottom of the PHT Tracing Test form and copy this final time (in seconds) to the PHT Scoring Sheet for this examinee (examinees should also record their own time on the PHT Scoring Sheet).

f.	Group members will then switch roles until everyone has administered and taken the test.

Step 5.	*Administer the PHT Dotting Test.*

a.	For the PHT Dotting Test, each group will need a watch, a sharpened pencil, and three copies of the test.

b.	To begin the test, the test administrator will read the following instructions <u>carefully</u>:
This is the Dotting Test for the PHT. When I say "GO!" you are to put one dot in each circle using your pencil as fast as you can. Begin at the first circle underneath "Start" and follow the string down and then up. Be careful when placing your dots as you will be penalized ½ second for each dot not placed in the circle. Ready, GO!

c.	After announcing the start of the test, the administrator will start timing the examinee using the stopwatch. When the examinee has reached the end of the test, immediately stop the stopwatch and record the time (in seconds) on the bottom of the PHT Dotting Test.

d.	Next, the administrator will carefully examine the dots drawn by the examinee. Circle any dots that are drawn either <u>on the circle</u> or

<u>outside of the circle</u>. Note the number of these mistakes on the PHT Dotting Test form.

    e.   Multiply the number of mistakes by ½ and add this number to the dotting test time. Write this final time on the bottom of the PHT Dotting Test and copy this final time (in seconds) to the PHT Scoring Sheet for this examinee (examinees should also record their own time on the PHT Scoring Sheet).

    f.   Group members will then switch roles until everyone has administered and taken the test.

Step 6.   *Administer the PHT Pursuit Test.*

    a.   For the PHT Pursuit Test, each group will need a watch, a sharpened pencil, and three copies of the test.

    b.   To begin the test, the test administrator will read the following instructions <u>carefully</u>:

This is the Pursuit Test for the PHT. Notice the numbers in the squares at the left where the curving lines begin. When I say "GO!" follow each line by eye from the square on the left where it begins to the square where it ends on the right. Remember the number at the beginning of the line on the left and put the same number in the square on the right. Do not use your pencil to follow the lines. Be careful when making your decisions as you will be penalized 2 seconds for each incorrect response. When you are finished with the test, announce "STOP!" to the administrator to stop the time. Ready, GO!

After announcing the start of the test, the administrator will start timing the examinee using the stopwatch. **Note***:* If the administrator has not yet taken the test, it is important that the administrator not watch the examinee complete the PHT Pursuit Test so that he or she does not see how the other examinees respond. When the examinee has reached the end of the test and announces "STOP," immediately stop the stopwatch and record the time (in seconds) on the bottom of the PHT Pursuit Test.

    c.   Group members will then switch roles until everyone has administered and taken the test. After everyone in the group has taken the PHT Pursuit Test, the administrator will then score the test. The correct answers for the PHT Pursuit Test (starting at the top and moving down) are as follows: **5, 7, 6, 2, 4, 8, 3, 1**

    d.   Circle any numbers that are not correct. Note the number of mistakes on the PHT Pursuit Test.

    e.   Multiply the number of mistakes by 2 and add this number to the pursuit test time. Write this final time on the bottom of the PHT Pursuit Test and copy this final time (in seconds) to the PHT Scoring Sheet for this examinee (examinees should also record their own time on the PHT Scoring Sheet).

Step 7.   *Gather class data and calculate averages.*

    a.   For each examinee, sum the total time across the four PHT subtests on the PHT Scoring Sheet.

    b.   Once all groups have finished the PHT, each group will share their data with the class. The instructor will write the times on the board and the class will calculate averages for each of the PHT subtests.

    c.   Record these averages in the last column of the PHT Scoring Sheet.

QUESTIONS

1.   Which of the physical ability tests was the easiest for you? Most difficult for you? Why?

2.   Compare your score on each subtest with the other members of your group and with the class average. How did you perform on the test compared to your group? Your class? If these tests were used to make a job selection decision, do you think you would have been selected?

3.   Considering the human abilities you believe each ability test measures, for what jobs might each test be useful in personnel selection and/or vocational counseling? How would you conduct a validity study to evaluate what abilities were really being measured by each of the tests?

PHT TRACING TEST

START

Tracing test time (in seconds): _____

Number of mistakes: _____ (add ½ second for each mistake)

Final tracing test time: _____

PHT DOTTING TEST

START

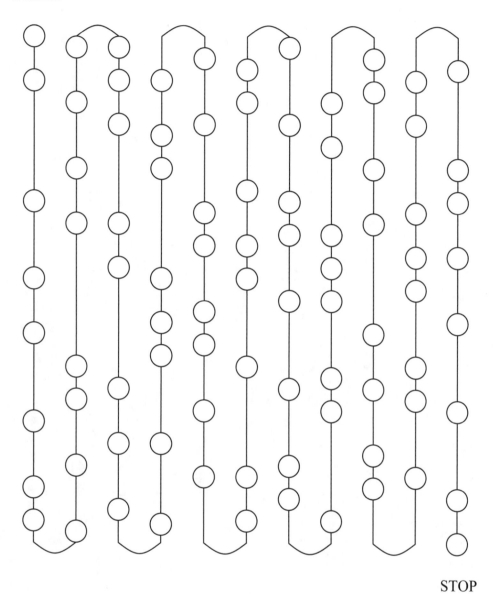

STOP

Dotting test time (in seconds): _____

Number of mistakes: _____ (add ½ second for each mistake)

Final dotting test time: _____

PHT PURSUIT TEST

Pursuit test time (in seconds): _____

Number of mistakes: _____ (add 2 seconds for each mistake)

Final pursuit test time: _____

PHT SCORING SHEET

PHT Subtest	Time to Complete Subtest			
	Examinee 1	Examinee 2	Examinee 3	Class Average
Sorting				
Tracing				
Dotting				
Pursuit				
Total Time				

EXERCISE 9
ADMINISTERING AND SCORING A ROLE PLAYING EXERCISE (RPE)

INTRODUCTION

As in the case of an in-basket simulation (Exercise #6), a role play exercise is a "real world" testing tool. It uses a social simulation to assess a person's responses. A role playing exercise is a common assessment approach when you want to see how a person is able to handle a situation in a specific social context (e.g., work, school). An examinee is asked to assume the role of a hypothetical person in order to judge if he/she is able to exhibit specific, desirable decision-making and/or behavior outcomes in response to a "real world" task. The examinee is then assessed on specific characteristics (e.g., leadership skill) and judged whether he/she is good at working with others. In a workplace setting, this type of testing would be used within a battery of tests (i.e., combination of tests) to identify candidates for hiring and/or promotion, or possibly for further training if deficiencies are noted.

This exercise demonstrates how to administer and score a role playing exercise as it would be used within a battery of tests for job candidate selection. Why use a "battery" of tests? Ensuring that the testing process (as well as the testing content) matches the job for which one is hiring is a major concern in employment testing. Why? The answer is fairness. For example, if the position being selected for primarily involves oral skills, but your testing process involves primarily writing skills, this would be unfair to candidates who are strong in oral skills but are rejected due to a poor writing skills score in the work sample. It is equally important for employers, as they are relying on HR departments to accurately assess candidates' job-related qualifications (e.g., communication skills).

The Role Playing Exercise (RPE) will be used as an example of an assessment center/work sample type exercise that assesses many important areas of interpersonal skills/behaviors and associated problem analysis and decision making capabilities inherent in choosing an effective employee. The specific focus of this exercise will be assessing potential candidates for the job of mid-level manager who supervises a division of 100-150 employees, both "line" workers and their immediate supervisors. The capabilities of the manager to deal with subordinates' issues of concern in the workplace (i.e., managerial effectiveness) will be assessed through the role playing exercise.

MATERIALS NEEDED

1	Copy of the Informed Consent Form Template (Appendix A)
2	Copies of the Universal Demographic Sheet (Appendix B)
1	Stopwatch or a watch with a second-hand
2	Sharp #2 pencils
2	Clean manila folders
2	Copies of the Role Playing Exercise (RPE) Instruction Sheet
1	Copy of Test Administrator's Role Play Script
2	Copies of the RPE Behavioral Observations Sheet
2	Copies of the RPE Individual Scoring Sheet
2	Copies of the RPE Self-rating Feedback Form
1	Copy of the Interpretive Guidelines
2	Copies of the Correlation Data Sheet and Computation (Appendix C)
1	Copy of the Computation of Student's *t* (Appendix D)

PROCEDURE

A. ADMINISTRATION

Step 1.   *Compose an Informed Consent Form.*

The class will create an informed consent form (Appendix A) to be given to all volunteer participants that will inform them of the nature and purpose of the exercise, and will reinforce the anonymity and confidentiality of any information requested.

Step 2.   *Prepare materials.*

     a.   In a manila folder for the examinee, place the following items in order from top to bottom:
- (1)   created Informed Consent Form,
- (2)   Universal Demographic Sheet (Appendix B), and
- (3)   RPE Instruction Sheet.

     b.   In a second manila folder for the test administrator, place the following items in order from top to bottom:
- (1)   Copy of Test Administrator's Role Play Script,
- (2)   Copy of the RPE Behavioral Observations Sheet,
- (3)   Copy of the RPE Self-rating Feedback Form, and
- (4)   Copy of the RPE Individual Scoring Sheet.

     c.   Assign a random ID # to each participant, and place that same number on all documents for each participant (i.e., on the Universal Demographic Sheet, the RPE Instruction Sheet, RPE Behavioral Observations Sheet, RPE Feedback Form, and RPE Individual Scoring Sheet).

Step 3.   *Review necessary information.*

Before recruiting participants,:

     a.   review both the Test Administrator's Role Play Script and RPE Behavioral Observations sheet so that you are familiar with the role play process and you are cognizant of which behaviors and characteristics to pay attention to during the session, and

     b.   review the RPE Individual Scoring Sheet so that you will remember what to record for scoring purposes.

Step 4.   *Recruit participants.*

Each class member will test two undergraduate college students. If possible, one person should be a Business or Theater Arts major and one person should be a different major than those listed. Information regarding college major will be collected on the Universal Demographic Sheet.

Step 5.	Introduce task.

    a.   Test each person individually, in a quiet, relatively distraction-free room.

    b.   Once the person is seated,:

        (1)   introduce yourself and give a general explanation of the task.

        (2)   give the person an Informed Consent Form to complete, and answer any questions that arise. Collect signed consent form and continue.

        (3)   give the participant a numbered Universal Demographic Sheet and ask them to complete it. Collect the completed form.

        (4)   answer any questions the participant might have before beginning the role play exercise.

Step 6.	Administer the RPE exercise.

    a.   Notify the participant that you will begin the role play exercise shortly, and briefly review again the contents of the Test Administrator's Role Play Script.

    b.   Reiterate to the participant that the activity simulates a role play exercise.

    c.   Begin the interview using the Test Administrator's Role Play Script as a guide. Present the role play "prompts" in exactly the order that they appear on the script.
Instruct the participant to:

        (1)   listen to each of role play suggestions carefully, and respond accordingly.

        (2)   adhere to the five-minute time limit for each response. Whether suggested by the participant or not, proceed to the next part of the role play exercise if five minutes has elapsed since the participant's role play response period began.

    d.   Continue this iterative process for the remaining parts of the role play exercise. End the role play exercise after either 30 minutes has elapsed or the participant has responded to all scripted prompts for scoring purposes.

Step 7.	Record responses.

Record both the oral responses, as well as the behavioral (non-verbal) responses, during the role play using both the RPE Individual Scoring Sheet and the RPE Behavioral Observations Sheet.

Step 8.	Obtain feedback.

Give the participant a numbered RPE Self-rating Feedback Form. Ask the person to use the scale provided to rate how well he/she did on the role play task.

B.   SCORING AND ANALYSIS
   Step 1.   *Score exercise.*
                     Assess each participant's "managerial effectiveness" dimension
                     performance in the role play task using the RPE Individual Scoring Sheet.
                     Add up the 5-point Likert scale ratings to derive a total score (Total RPE
                     Score). The following is the interpretation table for that score calculation
                     (also presented at end of the actual scoring form):

RPE Score Range Interpretation:
 5 - 9 points: Total RPE Score points = *poor* potential managerial effectiveness
10 - 14 points: Total RPE Score points = *below average* potential managerial effectiveness
15 - 19 points: Total RPE Score points = *average* potential managerial effectiveness
20 - 25 points: Total RPE Score points = *above average* potential managerial effectiveness

   Step 2.   *Record data.*
                     Each class member shall record the scores of the participants they tested
                     and the participants' own self-evaluation scores on the first line of the
                     appropriate Correlation Data Sheet (Appendix C). One sheet is used for
                     Business or Theater Arts majors and one sheet is used for "other" majors.

   Step 3.   *Combine class data.*
                     Class members will share their data with the rest of the class so that all
                     will have completed Correlation Data Sheets.

   Step 4.   *Correlate objective and subjective scores.*
                     Once all the performance scores for the class have been collected,
                     compute the correlation (Appendix C) between the self-evaluation scores
                     and the actual performance scores. Do this separately for the Business or
                     Theater Arts majors and for the "other" majors.

   Step 5.   *Investigate possible differences between groups.*
                     a.   Using the data from the "Business or Theater" major and "other
                              majors" groups, each class member will compute an independent
                              group's *t* test (Appendix D) to investigate the significance of the
                              difference between the RPE scores.
                     b.   Using a Table of Significance for *t*, class members will determine
                              the *p* value of the obtained *t* value (area in tail).

QUESTIONS
1.   What parts of the administration did you find the easiest? Hardest?

2.   What parts of the scoring did you find the easiest? Hardest?

3.   Which parts of the scoring seemed to involve the most subjectivity? Which parts seemed
     to be more objective?

RPE INSTRUCTION SHEET

Overview of exercise: You are a middle-level manager in a large corporation. This role play exercise will assess your responses to hypothetical workplace issues that managers typically encounter. In responding, simply go with your initial response and do not waste time attempting to "second guess" what would the test administrator expects.

Role play task: The test administrator will play the role of a subordinate whom you supervise. During the course of the exercise, the "subordinate" will present typical employee issues that need your decisions. Again, try to respond as you would in a normal workplace situation in the role of a supervising manager.

If you have any questions, ask them at this time. If not, please notify the rater that you are ready to begin.

TEST ADMINISTRATOR'S ROLE PLAY SCRIPT

Overview of exercise: You will play the role of a subordinate whom the test examinee supervises. The test examinee has been told to assume the role of a middle-level manager in a large corporation for purposes of the exercise. The examinee has been told that this role play exercise will assess his/her responses to hypothetical workplace issues that managers typically encounter. Further, the examinee has been instructed to go with his/her initial response and to not waste time attempting to "second guess" what would you (the rater) expect.

Role play task: During the course of the exercise, you will present typical employee issues that need decisions from the examinee. The proceeding is the script to be followed to elicit examinee's responses (please be sure to adhere to the wording of the script verbatim, and do not paraphrase, to maintain standardization of testing across examinees).

Script:

"Hello, my name is_____, and I am a newly-hired person in your division. You are my middle-level supervising manager. I just have a few issues to ask you about after my first week on the job."

[Wait for examinee's response to intro]

"The first issue I am concerned about was an incident that occurred on my first day. Specifically, a co-worker made me feel uncomfortable by grabbing me from behind and giving me a bear hug. I do not believe that this person was being anything other than friendly from their perspective but I do not wish it to happen again. What should be done?"

[Record both examinee's verbal and non-verbal responses to the issue to be addressed]

"Thank you for your advice! Unfortunately, I have more issues to discuss. Of great importance is the fact that I don't seem to get along with my immediate supervisor, Helen. She constantly criticizes my work. What should be done?"

[Record both examinee's verbal and non-verbal responses to the issue to be addressed]

"I have to admit that you have been a better listener than the VP of the company. I think I have e-mailed him about 25 times but have not received any response yet. Any advice?"

[Record both examinee's verbal and non-verbal responses to the issue to be addressed]

"I am kind of unclear about the company policy on 'Casual Friday.' I was thinking of wearing my pajamas because that is what I wear mostly on the weekends. Any advice?"

[Record both examinee's verbal and non-verbal responses to the issue to be addressed]

"I am paying attention to your advice. One more thing. I feel we have a real "connection" after speaking with you. Would you like to go get some coffee sometime?"

[Record both examinee's verbal and non-verbal responses to the issue to be addressed]

"Thanks! See you later!"

[End role play, and record any final examinee responses]

RPE INDIVIDUAL SCORING SHEET

ID#:_____

Response #1 ("bear hug" issue): _____

_____
_____
_____
_____
_____
_____
_____
_____
_____
_____
_____
_____

Overall *Managerial Effectiveness* level for response #1 (circle one):

1	2	3	4	5

Poor   Average   Very Good
(Did not respond)   (Defers problem to others)   (Addresses issue
directly, actively)

Response #2 ("critical supervisor" issue): _____

_____
_____
_____
_____
_____
_____
_____
_____
_____
_____
_____

Overall *Managerial Effectiveness* level for response #2 (circle one):

1	2	3	4	5

Poor   Average   Very Good
(Did not respond)   (Defers problem to others)   (Addresses issue
directly, actively)

Response #3 ("VP contact" issue): _____

_____

_____

_____

_____

_____

_____

_____

_____

_____

_____

Overall *Managerial Effectiveness* level for response #3 (circle one):

1	2	3	4	5

Poor   Average   Very Good
(Did not respond)   (Defers problem to others)   (Addresses issue
directly, actively)

Response #4 ("Casual Friday" issue): _____

_____

_____

_____

_____

_____

_____

_____

_____

_____

_____

Overall *Managerial Effectiveness* level for response #4 (circle one):

1	2	3	4	5

Poor   Average   Very Good
(Did not respond)   (Defers problem to others)   (Addresses issue
directly, actively)

Response #5 ("connection" issue): _____

_____
_____
_____
_____
_____
_____
_____
_____
_____
_____
_____

Overall *Managerial Effectiveness* level for response #5 (circle one):

1	2	3	4	5

Poor
(Did not respond)

Average
(Defers problem to others)

Very Good
(Addresses issue
directly, actively)

Total RPE Score = _____

RPE Score Range Interpretation:

5 - 9 points: Total RPE Score points = *poor* potential managerial effectiveness

10 - 14 points: Total RPE Score points = *below average* potential managerial effectiveness

15 - 19 points: Total RPE Score points = *average* potential managerial effectiveness

20 - 25 points: Total RPE Score points = *above average* potential managerial effectiveness

RPE BEHAVIORAL OBSERVATIONS SHEET

ID#:_____

BEHAVIORS DURING TESTING

1.   Appearance and posture:_____
     _____
     _____
     _____
     _____
     _____

2.   Overall attitude toward testing situation: _____
     _____
     _____
     _____
     _____
     _____

3.   Level and kind of emotions displayed: _____
     _____
     _____
     _____
     _____
     _____

4.   Noteworthy remarks made by participant during testing: _____
     _____
     _____
     _____
     _____
     _____

5.   Level of satisfaction expressed about performance: _____
     _____
     _____
     _____
     _____
     _____

6.   Additional comments: _____
     _____
     _____
     _____
     _____

RPE SELF-RATING FEEDBACK FORM

ID #: _____

On the following scale, rate how well you think you did on this role play exercise assessing your potential managerial effectiveness.

Circle the number that comes closest to your opinion of your role play exercise performance.

1	2	3	4	5
Very Poor	Poor	Average	Good	Very Good

Please explain self-rating:_____

_____

_____

_____

_____

_____

EXERCISE 10
ADMINISTERING AND SCORING AN
INTERVIEW ASSESSMENT SCALE (IAS)

INTRODUCTION

An interview is a relatively common assessment tool in many different contexts (e.g., work, school) to judge the characteristics of the person being interviewed. There are three basic forms of an interview structure format, ranging on a continuum from a relatively unscripted, spontaneous interview process (i.e., "unstructured interview" format) to a highly scripted, sequenced set of interview questions (i.e., "structured interview" format). A "semi-structured interview" format is a "middle ground" combination of the two other interview formats.

Structured interviews have attributes that are arguably beneficial to assessment. To have a clear, well-planned conceptualization of what will be asked, and how it relates to specific cognitive and/or behavioral dimensions of assessment, it is important for assessment to be properly conducted. Structured interviews allow for "control" in what can be asked and how it will be scored before the interview is ever done. From a legal perspective, for example, a structured interview is more desirable for employers because of its apparent "face validity" due to the standardization of the questions posed (hopefully job relevant) to all candidates, as well as its ability to establish good reliability and validity if well developed.

The present exercise will be focused on the administration and scoring of a structured behavioral interview format because of its relatively straightforward process and subsequent scoring. More specifically, the structured interview content will elicit responses to posed hypothetical social situations in order to assess motivations toward altruistic behavior (i.e., "helpfulness," "empathy," and "selflessness" sub dimension scores).

MATERIALS NEEDED

1   Copy of the Informed Consent Form Template (Appendix A)
2   Copies of the Universal Demographic Sheet (Appendix B)
1   Stopwatch or a watch with a second hand
2   Sharp #2 pencils
2   Clean manila folders
2   Copies of the IAS Interview Sheet
2   Copies of the IAS Behavioral Observations Sheet
2   Copies of the IAS Self-rating Feedback Form
2   Copies of the IAS Individual Scoring Sheet
2   Copies of the Correlation Data Sheet and Computation (Appendix C)
1   Copy of the Computation of Student's *t* (Appendix D)

PROCEDURE
A.   ADMINISTRATION

     Step 1.   *Compose an Informed Consent Form.*
                       The class will create an informed consent form (Appendix A) to be given to all volunteer participants that will inform them of the nature and purpose of the exercise, and will reinforce the anonymity and confidentiality of any information requested.

Step 2.   *Prepare materials.*

      a.   In a manila folder for the examinee, place the following items in order from top to bottom:

            (1)   created Informed Consent Form, and

            (2)   Universal Demographic Sheet (Appendix B).

      b.   In a second manila folder for the test administrator, place the following items in order from top to bottom:

            (1)   Copy of the IAS Interview Sheet,

            (2)   Copy of the IAS Behavioral Observations Sheet,

            (3)   Copy of the IAS Feedback Form, and

            (4)   Copy of the IAS Individual Scoring Sheet.

      c.   Assign a random ID # to each participant and place that same number on all documents for each participant on the Universal Demographic Sheet, IAS Interview Sheet, IAS Behavioral Observations Sheet, IAS Feedback Form, and IAS Individual Scoring Sheet.

Step 3.   *Recruit participants.*

Each class member will test two undergraduate college students. If possible, one person should be a Communications major and one person should be a non-Communications major (e.g., Social Work major). Information regarding college major will be collected on the Universal Demographic Sheet.

Step 4.   *Introduce task.*

      a.   Test each person individually, in a quiet, relatively distraction-free room.

      b.   Once the person is seated,:

            (1)   introduce yourself and give a general explanation of the task.

            (2)   give the person an Informed Consent Form to complete, and answer any questions that arise. Collect signed consent form and continue.

            (3)   give the participant a numbered Universal Demographic Sheet and ask him/her to complete it. Collect completed sheet.

            (4)   answer any questions the participant might have before beginning the interview.

Step 5.   *Administer the IAS exercise.*

      a.   Notify the participant that you will begin the interview shortly, and briefly review again the contents of the IAS Interview Sheet.

      b.   Reiterate to the participant that the exercise simulates a structured interview process.

c.   Begin the interview using the IAS Interview Sheet as a guide. Present the interview questions in exactly the order that they appear on the IAS Interview Sheet.

Script: *Please respond to the following interview scenarios. You will have five minutes to respond to each scenario. In responding, explain how you would react to each posed social situation. Do you have any questions before we begin?*

Instruct the participant to:

(1)   listen to each of the interview question carefully, and verbally suggest an action to be taken in each scenario posed.

(2)   adhere to the five-minute time limit for each response. Instruct the participant to indicate when he/she is ready to proceed to the next interview question or proceed to the next question if five minutes has elapsed since the response period began.

(3)   read aloud each scenario, and record interviewee's responses on the IAS Interview Sheet.

d.   Continue this iterative process for the remaining interview questions.

Step 6.   *Record responses.*
Record <u>both</u> the oral (verbal) and behavioral (non-verbal) responses during the interview using the IAS Behavioral Observations Sheet.

Step 7.   *Obtain feedback.*
Give the participant a numbered IAS Self-rating Feedback Form. Ask the person to use the scale provided to rate how well he/she did on the task.

B.   SCORING AND ANALYSIS

Step 1.   *Score exercise.*
Assess each participant's performance on the task using the IAS Individual Scoring Sheet.

Step 2.   *Record data.*
Each class member shall record the scores of the participants he/she tested and the participants' own evaluation scores on the first line of the appropriate Correlation Data Sheet (Appendix C). One sheet is used for Communication majors and one sheet is used for non-Communication majors.

Step 3.   *Combine class data.*
Class members will share their data with the rest of the class so that all will have completed Correlation Data Sheets.

Step 4.   *Correlate objective and subjective scores.*
Once all the performance scores for the class have been collected, compute the correlation (Appendix C) between the self-evaluation scores (subjective) and the actual performance (objective) scores. Do this separately for the Communication majors and for the non-Communication majors.

Step 5.   *Investigate possible differences between groups.*
  a.   Using the data from the "Communication" major and "non-Communication" major groups, each class member will compute an independent group's *t* test (Appendix D) to investigate the significance of the difference between the final total IAS rating scores.
  b.   Using a Table of Significance for *t*, class members will determine the *p* value of the obtained *t* value (area in tail).

QUESTIONS

1.   How well did the person's self-rating of IAS performance correlate with the actual IAS scores? If there is a low correspondence, why would there be?

2.   What were the results of the comparison of the mean scores between the Communication and non-Communication majors? What did you expect the results to be? Were your expectations supported?

3.   Based on your readings and what you learned through doing this exercise, how effective is this assessment approach? Explain your answer and integrate with class readings.

IAS INTERVIEW SHEET

Instructions to be read to the interviewee:
The following scenarios are to be responded to in the order presented. Please put yourself in the role of the respondent in each scenario, and offer a genuine reaction according to how you would react in each situation presented. Explain your thoughts and motivations in your responses to each scenario.

Scenario #1:

It is 10:32 a.m. on a Tuesday. You are running from work to another meeting, and you are very late for the meeting. You are getting into a Taxi when a total stranger grabs your arm and asks for directions. He appears to be anxious and lost. What would you do?

_____
_____
_____
_____
_____
_____
_____
_____
_____
_____
_____
_____

Scenario #2:

It is 7 a.m. on a Saturday. A neighbor knocks on your door at home and requests a car ride to a doctor's appointment. She explains that she is late due to oversleeping and missed her regular bus that goes to the doctor's office. What would you do?

_____
_____
_____
_____
_____
_____
_____
_____
_____
_____

Scenario #3:

It is 3 p.m. on a Sunday. You are shopping downtown for a birthday party that will begin in about one hour. You are worried that you may be late if you do not get going soon. As you cross an intersection, you see a total stranger collapse on the opposite sidewalk. There are many people standing around the person but none are noticeably responding. What would you do?

_____

_____

_____

_____

_____

_____

_____

_____

_____

_____

_____

Scenario #4:

It is 11 p.m. on a Thursday, and you are driving home from work. A total stranger calls your cell phone, asking for a person you do not know. The person sounds distraught on the line. You are then asked to look up the phone number of the person she is searching for. What would you do?

_____

_____

_____

_____

_____

_____

_____

_____

_____

_____

_____

Scenario #5:

It is 1:15 p.m. on a Wednesday. You are sitting in a local café, and just realize you are late for your next class. You see a textbook left on a nearby table as you get up to leave. You notice the group of people who just vacated the table is still standing outside on the sidewalk. What would you do?

_____

_____

_____

_____

_____

_____

_____

_____

_____

_____

_____

_____

_____

IAS BEHAVIORAL OBSERVATIONS SHEET

ID#:_____

BEHAVIORS DURING TESTING

1.   Appearance and posture: _____
_____
_____
_____
_____
_____

2.   Overall attitude toward testing situation: _____
_____
_____
_____
_____
_____

3.   Level and kind of emotions displayed: _____
_____
_____
_____
_____
_____

4.   Noteworthy remarks made by participant during testing: _____
_____
_____
_____
_____
_____

5.   Level of satisfaction expressed about performance: _____
_____
_____
_____
_____
_____

6.   Additional comments: _____
_____
_____
_____
_____

IAS SELF-RATING FEEDBACK FORM

ID #: _____

On the following scale, rate how well you think you did on this interview exercise assessing altruistic behavior.

Circle the number that comes closest to your opinion of your performance on the IAS exercise.

1	2	3	4	5
Very Poor	Poor	Average	Good	Very Good

Please explain self-rating:_____
_____
_____
_____
_____

IAS INDIVIDUAL SCORING SHEET

ID #: _____   FINAL TOTAL IAS RATING: _____

INSTRUCTIONS FOR IAS SCORING:

On this form, place a check (√) in front of those behaviors demonstrated in the participant's response (or lack thereof) to the items listed. The number(s) in parentheses after each behavior refer(s) to the relevant scenario number presented in the interview. The (+) or (-) before a behavior item indicates a positive or negative value placed on the occurrence of the Altruistic behavior (overall assessment across dimensions).

Dimension #1: "Helpfulness"   # of +'s _____   # of -'s _____

____+ Demonstrates willingness to help others (all scenarios)

____+ Responds to direct requests for assistance (Scenarios #1, #2, and #4)

____- Fails to help in unsolicited help situations (Scenarios #3 and #5)

____- Puts own interests/needs above others requesting/needing help (all scenarios)

Dimension #2: "Empathy"   # of +'s _____   # of -'s _____

____+ Offers a "calming" attitude/behavior in helping distressed "others" (all scenarios)

____+ Is emotionally responsive to help requests (e.g., expresses sadness) (scenarios #1, #2, and #4)

____- Expresses inability to identify with the person needing help (all scenarios)

____- Is unable to perceive and interpret "other's" needs in unsolicited help situations

Dimension #3: "Selflessness"   # of +'s _____   # of -'s _____

____+ Ignores own time demands/issues to help others (all scenarios)

____- Is unable to put needs of others ahead of own task demands/needs (all scenarios)

____- Sees conflict of goals between own needs and others' needs (all scenarios)

____+ Is willing to help others in a potentially "ego-threatening" social situation (scenarios #3 and #5)

OVERALL SCORING

Subtract the number of Minus (-) items checked from the number of Plus (+) items checked across the three sub dimensions to derive the overall "Altruistic" score.

    If the total difference obtained between Pluses and Minuses is:
    -6 to -5, Final Total Rating = 1
    -4 to -2, Final Total Rating = 2
    -1 to +1, Final Total Rating = 3
    +2 to +4, Final Total Rating = 4
    +5 to +6, Final Total Rating = 5

Using the guide below, rate the participant's overall performance on the overall test dimension "Altruism" (1 = Very Low to 5 = Very High).

Note: The verbal equivalents of these Final Total IAS Ratings are:

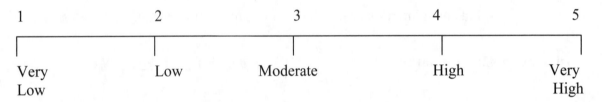

1	2	3	4	5
Very Low	Low	Moderate	High	Very High

Place this **Final Total IAS Rating** (both number score and verbal equivalent) at top of first page on this IAS Individual Scoring Sheet.

EXERCISE 11
BUILDING AN ACHIEVEMENT TEST
THE PSYCHOLOGY ACHIEVEMENT TEST (PAT)

INTRODUCTION

The IGAT and GGAT tests used in other exercises are modeled on a class of tests called "aptitude tests." These tests are intended to measure one's ability in a given area. In this exercise, we will turn our attention to a class of tests called "achievement tests," which are intended to measure how much learning has taken place.

The construction of achievement tests should follow a plan that assures adequate coverage of the material under consideration. This involves following a systematic procedure to make sure that the test is representative of all the relevant content. Items should also represent different types of knowledge. Two such types of knowledge, which will be used in this exercise, are the ability to remember factual material and the ability to apply information to a practical situation.

This exercise demonstrates several stages in the development of an achievement test covering basic knowledge from several areas of psychology. The Psychological Achievement Test (PAT) is to be used as an example of an academic achievement test that covers important areas in the field of psychology as identified by experts.

MATERIALS NEEDED

1	Copy of the Informed Consent Form Template (Appendix A)
2	Copies of the Universal Demographic Sheet (Appendix B)
1	Copy of the Areas Involved in the Topic of Psychology sheet
1	Copy of the PAT Tips for Writing Multiple Choice Questions
1	Copy of the PAT Model Chart for Test Item Distribution
1	Copy of the following materials:

> Study guides for General Psychology textbooks
> Preparation books for the Psychology CLEP examination
> Preparation books for the GRE Psychology Subject Test

1+	Copies of the PAT Group Data Sheet (data for 16 class members)
1	Copy of the PAT Statistical Summary Sheet
1	Copy of the Computation of Student's *t* (Appendix D)
1	Copy of Significance Table for *t-test* (from a Statistics text)

PROCEDURE
A. TEST PREPARATION

Step 1. *State the purpose of the test.*

Ordinarily, the class should reach a consensus about the desired purpose of this test. In this exercise, the purpose of the test will be to assess college students' knowledge of a wide variety of basic information about psychology. It might be used as an exit tool for an undergraduate program, as a criterion measure in studying the effectiveness of alternative teaching methods, or as a predictor of success for graduate school candidates.

Step 2.   *Select areas and sources for items.*
   a.   The class will review the Areas Involved in the Topic of Psychology sheet to see what areas are to be covered and with what emphasis.
   b.   The class will divide into work groups. Each group will choose a different content area to concentrate on when selecting and writing questions.

Step 3.   *Item selection and writing.*
   a.   Using the PAT Model Chart for Test Item Distribution sheet as a reference, each group will select the appropriate number of questions that should be written or selected from their area to create a 50-item initial version of the test.
   b.   The groups will select 2/3rds to 3/4ths of their items from sources such as:
        (1)   Internet sites.
        (2)   Study guides for General Psychology textbooks.
        (3)   Preparation books for the Psychology CLEP examination.
        (4)   Preparation books for the GRE Psychology Subject Test.
   c.   The groups will write the remaining items using the PAT Tips for Writing Multiple Choice Questions sheet as a reference. Each group should design at least two original questions.
   d.   Be sure you have the appropriate number of questions for each topic area and for each of the two types of knowledge. Using the PAT Model Chart to guide your writing and selection ensures giving appropriate coverage and is one step toward content validity.

Step 4.   *Collate data.*
   Each group will produce a list of multiple-choice questions, in the following format:

   (Item #)___.   (Stem of question goes here)_____.
                  A.   choice 1
                  B.   choice 2
                  C.   choice 3
                  D.   choice 4   Answer: Q # ___ = ____

   These lists should be typed with single spacing within the question and triple spacing in between questions so that questions may be cut apart.
   Sample item:
                  1.   Who is associated with using dream analysis in therapy?
                       A.   Erikson
                       B.   Watson
                       C.   Freud
                       D.   Levinson   Answer: Q #1 = C

Step 5.   *Create necessary additional test administration materials for the PAT.*
The class will form three work groups.

    a.   One group will create and type up an Informed Consent Form, using the Informed Consent Form Template (Appendix A) as a guide, and assuring participants of the privacy of their personal information. This step is not appropriate if you are using prepared data sets because the variables have already been chosen.

    b.   One group will create one set of instructions for the test taker and another set for the test administrator.

    c.   One group will take the lists of questions and:
        (1)   neatly cut the questions and the answers into strips,
        (2)   arrange the question strips in random order on pieces of paper, so that they can be photocopied as test forms;
        (3)   number the questions on the line preceding the stem, and
        (4)   create an answer key for the PAT.

B.   ADMINISTRATION

Step 1.   *Producing the preliminary version of the PAT.*

    a.   The class will design a first page for the test, with the following items:
        (1)   ID #.
        (2)   Relevant information chosen in *Step 5*a.
        (3)   Instructions for the examinee created in *Step 5*a.

    b.   The next pages are a photocopy of the pages created in *Step 5*c (2) and (3).

    c.   The last page is a copy of the answer key created in *Step 5*c (4).

Step 2.   *Make sufficient copies.*

    a.   Each class member will make a copy of the answer key for his or her own use.

    b.   Each class member will make three copies of the completed PAT for administration.

Step 3.   *Administering the preliminary version of the PAT.*
Each class member should administer the test to two students who are at different levels in the major and to one "expert" in the topic area (e.g., faculty members, graduate students). The student testing may be done individually or in a group.

Step. 4.   *Record results.*

    a.   Class members will use the created answer key to score the tests they administered.

    b.   The class will decide on which demographic item is to be recorded in which column and each class member will record the name at the top of the appropriate column of his/her copy of the PAT Group Data Sheet (Info# 1, #2, #3, #4).

    c.   Each class member will use the first lines of the appropriate section of the PAT Group Data Sheets to record each participant's information and scores that includes columns for the demographic items selected as relevant; the expert data section only includes ID and the PAT score.

C.   ANALYSIS

Step 1.   *Collate the data.*

Class members will share their data so that every person will have a completed copy of the PAT Group Data Sheet.

Step 2.   *Compute descriptive statistics.*

    a.   Each student should compute the Mean and Standard Deviation for:

        (1)   Students only.

        (2)   Experts only.

        (3)   The whole group.

    b.   Transfer the results to the PAT Statistical Summary Sheet.

Step 3.   *Collate the data.*

Groups will share their correlation results with the class so that everyone will have a completed PAT Statistical Summary Sheet.

Step 4.   *Compute the difference statistic.*

    a.   Using the data from the student and expert groups, each class member will compute an independent group's *t* test (Appendix D) to investigate the significance of the difference between the PAT scores.

    b.   Using a Table of Significance for *t*, class members will determine the *p* value of the obtained *t* value (area in tail).

    c.   Transfer the results to the PAT Statistical Summary Sheet (you could use the answer key for the GGAT as a model).

QUESTIONS

1. How does this test differ from tests like the IGAT or the GGAT?

2. Would you expect the scores on the PAT to change or remain stable over time? Why or why not?

3. What did you learn about writing test items? What was the hardest part of the item writing process? The easiest?

AREAS INVOLVED IN THE TOPIC OF PSYCHOLOGY

Use These Guideline Percentages to Determine Number of Questions Needed in that Category

Physiology and Behavior	8%
Sensation and Perception	9%
Motivation and Emotion	11%
Learning	14%
Cognition	7%
Life-span Development	10%
Personality and Adjustment	12%
Behavioral Disorders	9%
Social Psychology	10%
Measurement and Statistics	7%
History and Philosophy	3%

PAT TIPS FOR WRITING MULTIPLE CHOICE QUESTIONS

1. Each question should contain only one main idea.

2. Item stem and all of the alternative answers should be grammatically compatible.

3. Items should be expressed in precise language.

4. Avoid irrelevant sources of difficulty in the stem (e.g., difficult vocabulary and jargon).

5. Use negatively worded items sparingly and when you do, set off the negative aspect by underlining or capitalizing the word that indicates negation (e.g., "not," "NOT").

6. Avoid the use of words such as "always" and "never." People usually over-interpret these kinds of questions since hardly anything in psychology is absolute.

7. Offer four response choices. One will be the correct, while the other three will be incorrect alternatives.

8. Make the incorrect alternative answers plausible.

9. Make the alternative answers of equal length so they are equally attractive to the reader.

10. Avoid alternative answers such as "All of the above." or "None of the above." Once a respondent knows that two of the choices apply, he/she automatically knows that the "all" or "none" response is the correct choice.

PAT MODEL CHART FOR TEST ITEM DISTRIBUTION

AREA OF PSYCHOLOGY AND PERCENT OF COVERAGE TO BE USED IN TEST	TOTAL NUMBER OF QUESTIONS	NUMBER OF KNOWLEDGE QUESTIONS	NUMBER OF APPLICATION QUESTIONS
Physiology and Behavior (8%)	4	2	2
Sensation and Perception (9%)	4	2	2
Motivation and Emotion (11%)	5	3	2
Learning (14%)	7	4	3
Cognition (7%)	4	2	2
Life-span Development (10%)	5	3	2
Personality and Adjustment (12%)	6	4	2
Behavioral Disorders (9%)	5	3	2
Social Psychology (10%)	5	3	2
Measurement and Statistics (7%)	3	2	1
History and Philosophy (3%)	2	1	1
TOTALS (100%)	50	29	21

PAT GROUP DATA SHEET

STUDENT DATA						EXPERT DATA	
ID #	INFO #1	INFO #2	INFO #3	INFO #4	PAT SCORE	ID#	PAT SCORE

PAT STATISTICAL SUMMARY SHEET

<u>Student</u> Statistics

     Mean of PAT Scores   _____

     S.D. of PAT Scores   _____

<u>Expert</u> Statistics

     Mean of PAT Scores   _____

     S.D. of PAT Scores   _____

<u>Whole Group</u> Statistics

     Mean of PAT Scores   _____

     S.D. of PAT Scores   _____

Difference Statistic between <u>Students</u> and <u>Experts</u>

     $t =$ _____

     $p =$ _____

EXERCISE 12
EMPIRICAL CONSTRUCTION OF SCALES
THE ACADEMIC ORIENTATION TEST (AOT)

INTRODUCTION

Many personality and vocational interest tests used in diagnostic and counseling settings are constructed by means of discovering the thoughts, behaviors, attitudes, or emotions that are more common to one group of people than to another. Their use provides the clinician or the counselor with a standardized method for categorizing individuals or for guiding them into fields that will suit them the best. The technique used for creating these kinds of tests is called "empirical scale construction." In order to understand the procedures involved in this technique, this exercise will involve creating a questionnaire that differentiates members of four different undergraduate majors. In order to do this, the items on the Academic Orientation Test (AOT) should reflect the relatively unique pattern of activities, preferences, and behaviors associated with persons in each of the four undergraduate major categories.

The class members as a whole will first create a list of characteristics that they think are descriptive of each of the different major groups and then, using this list for reference, will construct a preliminary version of the AOT. Each student in the class will then administer this preliminary AOT to friends or acquaintances who are either in college or have gone to college to confirm the interests and frequent behaviors for each of the four major categories. Some of the preliminary version questionnaires administered will be used to establish norms, while others will be used to check the scoring procedure.

MATERIALS NEEDED

1	Copy of the Informed Consent Form Template (Appendix A)
2	Copies of the Universal Demographic Sheet (Appendix B)
1	Copy of the AOT Criterion Groups Characteristics Sheet
1	Copy of the AOT Criterion Groups Characteristics Worksheet
1	Copy of the AOT Possible Test Items Pool sheet
1	Copy of the AOT Template Sheet
1	Copy of the 4-page AOT Item Selection Worksheet
12	Copies of the AOT Item Response Sheets
1	Copy of the AOT Scoring Keys
1	Copy of the AOT Group Data Sheet (for every five members in the class)
1	Copy of the AOT Percentile Norms Tables

✓ If needed, complete sample AOT scale of 60 items is available on the accompanying CD-Rom (*E12_AOT_Scale.doc*).
✓ If needed, Based on pilot testing with past lab students, a percentage table is provided on the accompanying lab manual CD-Rom (*E12_AOT_Responses.doc*).

PROCEDURE

A. CONSTRUCTION OF PRELIMINARY AOT

Step 1. *Compose an Informed Consent Form.*
The class will create an informed consent form (Appendix A) to be given to all volunteer participants that will inform them of the nature and purpose of the exercise, and will reinforce the anonymity and confidentiality of any information requested.

Step 2. *Identification of criterion groups.*
For this exercise, the criterion groups will be students with majors in Fine Arts, Humanities, Social Sciences, and Natural Sciences. The scale that is to be constructed will attempt to differentiate between each of these criterion (major) groups on the one hand and a group of students-in-general on the other. In order for this exercise to work, the class members must select examinees with well-defined major preferences as members of the four criterion groups.

Step 3. *Delineation of criterion characteristics.*
The class will discuss the probable characteristics (e.g., personality traits, talents, likes and dislikes) of the different groups until they have as clear a picture as possible of the individuals they will ask to participate. Using the AOT Criterion Groups Characteristics Sheet as a starting point, and adding to or deleting from it, they will complete the AOT Criterion Groups Characteristics Worksheet. The items on this Worksheet should be the product of consensus.

Step 4. *Select items for preliminary AOT.*
a. The class members will use the AOT Possible Items Pool as a reference.
b. One class member (or the instructor) will act as a recorder by making eight columns on the blackboard, two columns for each major.
c. The first column for each major shall be labeled "agree." The class shall select those statements with which a student from that major category would likely agree. The second column shall be labeled "disagree" and will contain those statements with which the same students would likely disagree. Rather than writing out the entire sentence, the recorder will enter each statement's corresponding item # in the appropriate columns (either "agree" or "disagree" column).
d. Class members should also create items to cover characteristics that are in the list of characteristics for a given major, but are not addressed by any of the statements provided.
e. There should be a total of 15 question numbers, including created questions, for each of the four major groups to create a 60-item, first version of the AOT.

Step 5.   *Create test format for preliminary AOT.*

    a.   The class will divide into four groups. Each group will take one set of 15 questions and type them single spaced within the items, triple spaced between the items, and in a "True/False" format. See the AOT Template Sheet Part A for a sample format for the question items.

    b.   The groups will randomize the order of the statements. Using a table of random numbers, group #1 will select 15 unique numbers between 1 and 60 for their 15 questions. The second group will repeat the process using the remaining 45 unique numbers. This process is repeated for the 3rd and 4th groups. Use Parts B and C of the AOT Template Sheet to organize the first and last pages of the document.

    c.   Cut the questions apart with even edges.

    d.   Place the question strips in numerical order on pieces of paper to make a preliminary AOT.

Step 6.   *Make copies of Preliminary AOT.*
Sufficient copies of the completed questionnaire should be made, so that each student has eight copies for administration.

Step 7.   *Choose option of existing AOT scale.*
For a less time-consuming option, a complete sample AOT scale of 60 items is provided on the accompanying lab manual CD-Rom. The MS Word file is entitled "*E12_AOT_Scale.doc*" on the CD-Rom.

B.   ADMINISTRATION OF PRELIMINARY AOT

Step 1.   *Administer the test to the criterion groups.*

    a.   Each student should locate two people who clearly identify themselves with each of the criterion groups (Total = eight participants) and administer the Informed Consent Form, Universal Demographic Sheet (Appendix B), and AOT to each participant. This may be done individually or in a group. In asking participants to volunteer, be careful not to divulge how you expect the participant to respond.

    b.   Instructions to use when administering test:
We are interested in your personal opinion about the following statements; there are no right or wrong answers. Indicate (T)rue or (F)alse before each statement. Please do not skip any items.

Step 2.   *Administer the test to the students-in-general group.*

    a.   Class members should each test four students who are undecided or feel they are interested in two or more areas. One possible source for this group would be freshman classes where the majority of enrolled students are undecided.

        b.   Instructions to use when administering the test are the same as in Part B *Step 1*.

Step 3.   *Record the results.*

        a.   Class members will transfer the responses of their participants to an AOT Item Response Record Sheet.

        b.   Using a different copy for each person, be sure to indicate at the top of the sheet the name of the group to which the participant belongs.

        c.   An alternative to doing steps 3.a. and 3.b., especially for those who may be working on the task individually or are not able to administer the test, would be to utilize an existing worksheet with past percentages of individuals from each of the four major groups who answered "True" to each of the 60 questions. This "short cut" option permits lab students to still go through the item selection process to create the scale. Based on pilot testing with past lab students, this percentage table is provided on the accompanying lab manual CD-Rom. The MS Word document is entitled "*E12_AOT_Responses.doc*" on the CD-Rom.

C.   ITEM SELECTION

Step 1.   *Selection of those questionnaires to use in item selection.*
Each student should select one of the AOT Item Response Record Sheets from each of the criterion group member surveys and two from his/her "students-in-general" respondents for the class to use in the item selection process.

Step 2.   *Form work groups.*

        a.   Five work groups will be formed, one for each major category and one for the "students-in-general" category.

        b.   Each class member will distribute his or her AOT Item Response Record Sheets to the appropriate groups.

Step 3.   *Tabulation of responses to the individual items.*
Each of the five work groups will:

        a.   count the number of "True" responses to each of the items and enter this in the appropriate "No." column of the AOT Item Selection Worksheets.

        b.   compute the percentage of students who responded "True" to each item (% = No. of true / total # of participants), and enter this in the appropriate "%" column of the AOT Item Selection Worksheets.

Step 4.   *Collate data.*
The students-in-general group will share its data so that all class members may complete that section of their AOT Item Selection Worksheets.

Step 5.   *Form new work groups.*
Class members who worked on the "students-in-general" data will now become members of one of the four major groups.

Step 6.   *Selection of items that differentiate.*
To identify which items belong on the various scales:
For each item of the major scale, subtract the percent responding "True" in the students-in-general group from the percent responding "True" in the particular subject area group and enter this number into the column labeled with a delta triangle (i.e., "Δ") on the AOT Item Selection Worksheets. The plus (+) or minus (-) sign should be recorded because this shows the direction of the difference.

Step 7.   *Creation of revised list of items.*
In actual test construction, statistics would be calculated indicating the probability that the obtained difference could have occurred by chance. These probabilities would be used to choose items that differentiate among the major groups. For this exercise, however, each work group should pick 10 items for each of the four major groups in order of the degree of relationship, starting with the largest deltas (Δ).

Step 8.   *Create Percentile Norms Tables.*
a.   For each of the 10 statements chosen, the "major" group will share with the rest of the class the:
(1)   original item number, and
(2)   direction of the answer to the item ("True" or "False").

b.   Each class member will put this information into the columns of the appropriate AOT Scoring Key. This data will be used in scoring the norm group.
There may be items that differentiate in the same way for more than one group. It is permissible to place one item on two scales; for example, the same item may indicate both Humanities and Social Science orientation. It would be undesirable if two scales had more than three or four items in common. If a large number of items (say over 50 percent) are on two scales, they are not measuring separate constructs, and the result will be too high a correlation between the scales.

D.   OBTAINING NORM GROUP DATA
Step 1.   *Scoring the norm group scales.*
After the items on each scale are identified, the questionnaires of a norming group should be scored. The norming group for this exercise will be the other six questionnaires each student has given.
a.   Class members will score their own six tests, using only the item numbers that are used in the AOT Scoring Keys. They will score

each questionnaire four times, once for each major group key. Each time they will use the numbered statements from a different one of the four major group keys created. Thus, each of the six norm group questionnaires will receive four scores, one score for each of the four major group scales.

b. The score on each scale is the number of items that the person answered in the same way as did the criterion group. A large number of "right" (i.e., keyed) answers results in a high score and indicates many responses like those of that criterion group.

c. Place the number "right" for each criterion group at the bottom of the last page of the questionnaire. Use the format:

$$F = \underline{\hspace{1cm}}; H = \underline{\hspace{1cm}}; N = \underline{\hspace{1cm}}; S = \underline{\hspace{1cm}}$$

d. Transfer these four scores to the first four lines of the AOT Group Data Sheet.

Step 2. *Collate data.*
Each class member will share their data so that the rest of the class can have completed AOT Group Data Sheets. Place a letter (F, H, N, or S) behind the ID# of those norm group participants who are majors in a given subject area.

Step 3. *Calculation of percentile norms.*
a. The class will divide into work groups, and each group will assume responsibility for computing percentiles for one of the major groups on the AOT Group Data Sheet (F, H, N, and S).

b. For each possible score of the scale assigned, the groups will compute:
(1) The number of students obtaining each of the possible scores, from 10 to 0. This number goes in column 2 of the appropriate Percentile Norms Table.
(2) The proportion of the total norm group achieving each particular score. This number goes in column 3 of the appropriate Percentile Norms Table.
(3) The score percentage for each score from 10 to 0. This number goes in column 4 of the appropriate Percentile Norms Table.
(4) The cumulative percentile (or percentile rank). The cumulative percentile is calculated by adding from the bottom up the score percentage for each possible score (0 to 10). This number goes in column 5 of the appropriate AOT Percentile Norms Table.

Step 4.   *Collate data.*
Groups will share their data so that everyone will have a completed set of AOT Percentile Norms Tables.

Step 5.   *Cross-validation.*
In "real world" test development, the revised scale would be administered to a new group of participants from the four major groups and scored on the scoring keys in order to see if the test correctly identifies the groups. This step is optional.

QUESTIONS

1. Which of your scales had the most number of items that showed a positive delta number only for that scale? How many items had negative delta values?

2. In the norming group, look at each group of majors (the lettered ID's) (see Part D, *Step 2*). How did the majors score on their own scale versus the other three scales? What does this tell you about the ability of the AOT to differentiate between groups?

3. Examine the content of the final items on each scale. Are there any items that don't "make sense" (i.e., ones that you would not have expected to show up on that scale)? What is the advantage of items that do not have face validity?

AOT CRITERION GROUPS CHARACTERISTICS SHEET

F = Fine Arts (e.g., Painting, Music, Dance)

Personal expression is important for these people. They feel that the arts have much to contribute to the betterment of the human condition.

H = Humanities (e.g., Literature, Philosophy, Linguistics, Languages)

These people love words. They are avid readers and enjoy interpreting what they read. They like working with concepts and ideas and enjoy discussing them with others.

N = Natural Sciences (e.g., Chemistry, Physics, Biology, Mathematics)

These people enjoy the challenge of difficult intellectual pursuits. They like to understand how things work, and math is not a problem for them. They tend to be more interested in physical matter than in people, so they do not mind working alone.

S = Social Sciences (e.g., Psychology, Sociology, Anthropology, History)

These people study human behavior from many different points of view. They try to understand why people behave in certain ways.

DESCRIPTORS	FINE ARTS	HUMANITIES	NATURAL SCIENCES	SOCIAL SCIENCES
A. Personality				
1.				
2.				
3.				
4.				
B. Talents				
1.				
2.				
3.				

AOT CRITERION GROUPS CHARACTERISTICS WORKSHEET   Page 1

AOT CRITERION GROUPS CHARACTERISTICS WORKSHEET   Page 2

DESCRIPTORS	FINE ARTS	HUMANITIES	NATURAL SCIENCES	SOCIAL SCIENCES
C. Work/Study Style				
1.				
2.				
3.				
4.				
D. Hobbies				
1.				
2.				
3.				

AOT POSSIBLE TEST ITEMS POOL

INSTRUCTIONS FOR USING THIS SHEET

The class will collectively choose 60 items for the preliminary form. These 60 items should be divided into 4 sets of 15 that might be considered relevant for each of the criterion groups. Choose items that a group would disagree with, as well as items that they would agree with. If there are characteristics you choose that are not covered in these items, write items to cover these characteristics.

T	F	1.	In high school I preferred my Biology class to my English class.
T	F	2.	Psychotherapy is not much different from witchcraft.
T	F	3.	Soft, fluffy, summer clouds inspire my creativity.
T	F	4.	I balance my checkbook every month.
T	F	5.	I would rather go to the Art Institute than to the Museum of Science and Industry.
T	F	6.	Painters of landscape and still life tend to be neurotic and isolated people.
T	F	7.	A person who doesn't enjoy detective television shows is missing an important part of life.
T	F	8.	I would rather read a novel than a science magazine.
T	F	9.	Children learn a lot by playing social games.
T	F	10.	People who are mentally ill should be locked up.
T	F	11.	Murals on buildings aren't really art, they just invite graffiti.
T	F	12.	I can't imagine why people would read a book if they could see the same story as a movie.
T	F	13.	Family dramas like *Providence* are much more interesting than science programs like *Nova*.
T	F	14.	Helping others is an important goal in my career of choice.
T	F	15.	Studying different cultures is a good way to learn more about ourselves.
T	F	16.	Artists should be honored and funded by society so they can have the freedom to be creative.
T	F	17.	Ballet and modern dancing contribute nothing to the welfare of society.
T	F	18.	People often go to college just to avoid going to work.
T	F	19.	It is better to like your job than to earn a lot of money.
T	F	20.	Experience is usually your best teacher.
T	F	21.	The study of the mind is just as important as the study of the body.
T	F	22.	Self expression is a most important form of communication.
T	F	23.	Educated people are much brighter than the average person.
T	F	24.	A man who does manual labor all his life is not very intelligent.
T	F	25.	What people learn in college will not be of use to them in the real world.
T	F	26.	There are too many science courses required in the average college program.
T	F	27.	Social scientists are the ones who can really make the world a better place.
T	F	28.	The mind and the body are two separate things.
T	F	29.	Psychological theories for raising children are usually just some author's personal opinion.
T	F	30.	I would rather listen to a symphony than surf the internet.

T	F	31.	People who do not appreciate the fine arts are ignorant, uneducated, or both.
T	F	32.	Science contributes more to human happiness than artistic creations do.
T	F	33.	I believe that young women go to college just to find a husband.
T	F	34.	Calculus, physics, and chemistry do not scare me.
T	F	35.	The government spends too much money on the space program.
T	F	36.	Scientific studies that have no practical applications are a waste of money.
T	F	37.	Mental illness could be cured if people had the will to control themselves.
T	F	38.	Poets contribute nothing to society.
T	F	39.	Unless you want to be a doctor or lawyer, there is no real reason to go to college.
T	F	40.	Monopoly is more fun than chess.
T	F	41.	I prefer a ball game to a concert.
T	F	42.	I like to play chess.
T	F	43.	I like difficult logical puzzles better than crossword puzzles.
T	F	44.	I watch TV for pleasure more often than I read books.
T	F	45.	After studying for a while, I have to go talk to someone before I can concentrate again.
T	F	46.	Even as a child, I enjoyed earning my own money.
T	F	47.	I enjoy the laboratory portions of science classes.
T	F	48.	I have many friends.
T	F	49.	In grammar school I preferred social studies over science.
T	F	50.	I have only one or two close friends.
T	F	51.	I have always been good at managing money.
T	F	52.	I enjoy finding ways to work with other people during group activities.
T	F	53.	I consider myself very organized.
T	F	54.	I would rather work with numbers than words.
T	F	55.	I am comfortable handling new situations.
T	F	56.	I enjoy watching people when I'm out in public.
T	F	57.	I prefer spending time with animals verses spending time with people.
T	F	58.	I buy a new book or magazine almost every week.
T	F	59.	I believe every group needs a strong leader.
T	F	60.	I can usually put things together by reading the directions.
T	F	61.	I like to exercise just for the fun of it.
T	F	62.	Life is a challenge.
T	F	63.	I would rather grab a quick snack than sit over a long meal with friends.
T	F	64.	Modern art is a reflection of confused minds.
T	F	65.	I am interested in the ways different groups do things, like raising families or conducting business.
T	F	66.	I treasure my time alone.
T	F	67.	I believe that anyone should be able to fix a lamp switch.
T	F	68.	I have donated to a wildlife or environmental organization.
T	F	69.	I do not have the time to read everything I want to.
T	F	70.	In my next life I want to return as a carpenter.
T	F	71.	Getting in good physical shape is high on my list of priorities.
T	F	72.	I would rather vacation in the mountains than take a cruise.

T	F	73.	I usually buy things on sale.
T	F	74.	I would choose a biography over a fiction novel.
T	F	75.	I would rather paint my walls myself than hire someone else to do it.
T	F	76.	When snacking, I'd choose a candy bar over an apple.
T	F	77.	If a button pulled off my coat, I would sew it back on.
T	F	78.	I am interested in finding out why people act the way they do.
T	F	79.	Exercise is important for its psychological effects.
T	F	80.	I encourage recycling projects.
T	F	81.	I like to browse through hardware stores.
T	F	82.	My friends consider me a good listener.
T	F	83.	I like to find new combinations in clothes.
T	F	84.	Even though I know that physical exercise would be good for me, I just do not have time for it.
T	F	85.	I like the idea of tracing my family's genealogy.
T	F	86.	When my sink gets stopped up, I call someone to fix it.
T	F	87.	When I'm at a picnic with a group of friends I would join in if they started a volleyball game.
T	F	88.	I believe it is important to know the background of an event in order to understand it.
T	F	89.	I like a number of different types of music.
T	F	90.	I think having people work for welfare money is a good idea.
T	F	91.	I dislike seeing anyone wearing a fur coat.
T	F	92.	I believe people's surroundings affect how they feel.
T	F	93.	I would be willing to pay extra for an energy-efficient home.
T	F	94.	I believe the government should emphasize public transportation to reduce the need for automobiles.
T	F	95.	When possible, I like to do things for myself.
T	F	96.	If I had to choose, I would more likely read *People* magazine rather than *Time*.
T	F	97.	I enjoy using the computer.
T	F	98.	I believe that store-bought things are better than home-made.
T	F	99.	Libraries bore me.
T	F	100.	I do not object to eating red meat more than four times a week.
T	F	101.	It upsets me to find that sports are about the only things appearing on Sunday afternoon television.
T	F	102.	I would rather eat a seven course meal than to expend energy exercising.
T	F	103.	I read the newspaper regularly.
T	F	104.	I enjoy finding out about new people.
T	F	105.	I would like to do research for a career.
T	F	106.	I'd rather read an interesting book than watch TV.
T	F	107.	I prefer investing in the stock market to putting my money in a savings account.
T	F	108.	I read many of the editorials in the newspaper.
T	F	109.	Most of my wardrobe is color-coordinated.
T	F	110.	I know what my weight is to within a few pounds.
T	F	111.	If I had a choice at my job, I would join a union.

T	F	112.	Even as a child, I always wanted to know how things worked.
T	F	113.	If I had the money, I would travel in order to find out how other cultures live.
T	F	114.	I have a favorite author.
T	F	115.	I usually wait for an elevator rather than use the stairs, even for going up one floor.
T	F	116.	I enjoy keeping my car in the best possible condition.
T	F	117.	I feel I get enough fiber in my diet without adding more.
T	F	118.	I believe that doctors should be better trained in nutrition and health.
T	F	119.	People who get ahead are a lot luckier than others.
T	F	120.	I spend too much time trying to find things I have mislaid.
T	F	121.	It is important for me to be active in my community.
T	F	122.	I keep an up-to-date phone number directory.
T	F	123.	I view each day as an opportunity for new adventures.
T	F	124.	With so much good music around there is no reason why I should learn to play a musical instrument.
T	F	125.	I believe that my life is largely predetermined.
T	F	126.	When I have time I like to do crossword puzzles.
T	F	127.	My class notes are usually not clearly labeled according to each class.
T	F	128.	I prefer a job where I am in charge and free to set my own goals and deadlines.
T	F	129.	When I shop I remember to buy everything I need.
T	F	130.	If my ideas were put to use the world would be a better place.
T	F	131.	When I take a Scantron test I often have to borrow a pencil.
T	F	132.	I would never cook a meal from "scratch" if prepared food was available.
T	F	133.	I have been known to blame a teacher when I did poorly on an exam.
T	F	134.	I envy a person who can write a good story.
T	F	135.	Without lucky breaks one cannot be successful.
T	F	136.	I have a special place for storing everything I have.
T	F	137.	I don't mind when people ask me for advice.
T	F	138.	I am often late and sometimes miss appointments.
T	F	139.	I always vote because I feel that my opinions might make a difference.
T	F	140.	I make my bed almost every morning.
T	F	141.	I sometimes check astrology charts to find out what my day will be like.
T	F	142.	When I do things with other people I often have good ideas to help out.
T	F	143.	I often wait until the last minute to study for exams.
T	F	144.	If I am faced with a problem, I will tend to ask for advice from others rather than trying to solve it myself.
T	F	145.	People are not likely to describe me as being clever.
T	F	146.	What happens to people in life is largely determined by how they plan and act.
T	F	147.	I don't think I could ever learn to paint a good original oil painting.
T	F	148.	My clothes are not always arranged in such a way that I know what I can wear.
T	F	149.	If I found someone sitting in my seat at a school play, I would find another seat.

T	F	150.	I don't mind if I have to be rude to a salesperson.
T	F	151.	I tend to feel distrustful of someone who does something nice for me.
T	F	152.	I am rarely comfortable in a crowd.
T	F	153.	I think most people agree that if you can't say something nice about someone, you should not say anything.
T	F	154.	When I lose a few coins in a vending machine I try to get a refund.
T	F	155.	When people disturb me by talking during a movie, I ask them to be quiet.
T	F	156.	Even if my steak wasn't prepared exactly as I ordered it, I would eat it anyway.
T	F	157.	I usually say the first thing that comes to my head.
T	F	158.	I tend to take people at their word.
T	F	159.	I have a fairly small group of acquaintances.
T	F	160.	If a co-worker accidentally spilled hot cocoa on me I would ask him or her to pay the cleaning bill.
T	F	161.	If a new date cancels "because of illness," I am suspicious.
T	F	162.	If I found that I was slightly overcharged at a grocery store, I would call the store to complain.
T	F	163.	I do not like spending much time alone if I can avoid it.
T	F	164.	I think that people are generally good.
T	F	165.	If a person cuts me off while driving, I would honk at him/her.
T	F	166.	I often think about the meaning of ideas such as beauty, truth, and joy.
T	F	167.	I have thought about joining a political club or committee.
T	F	168.	In a movie I prefer character development to special effects.
T	F	169.	When I am waiting in a line I often talk to other people who are also waiting.
T	F	170.	When I come across a word that is new to me, I look it up.
T	F	171.	In a group of people I am usually more quiet than the others.
T	F	172.	I nearly always run yellow lights to avoid having to stop.
T	F	173.	I often arrange get-togethers with other people.
T	F	174.	If I found a person was talking about me behind my back, I would ignore it.
T	F	175.	People who leave their coats unattended in a restaurant are likely to have them stolen.
T	F	176.	If I voice an opinion different from my friends' I wonder if they will stop liking me.
T	F	177.	If a teacher ran overtime in a class preceding another class in which I was having a test, I would just leave.
T	F	178.	I prefer to work by myself rather than with other people.
T	F	179.	I feel I have better than average creativity.
T	F	180.	I would describe myself as an extrovert.

AOT TEMPLATE SHEET

A. Question Format:

Put Your Chosen Items Into The Following Format:

T   F   In high school I preferred my Biology class to my English class.

T   F   Psychological theories for raising children are usually just some author's personal opinion.

T   F   Psychotherapy is not much different from witchcraft.

B. Front Page Format:

INTEREST AND ATTITUDE INVENTORY

Instructions: We are interested in your personal opinion about the following statements; there are no right or wrong answers.
Circle (T)rue or (F)alse before each statement. Please do not skip any items.

C. Last Page Format:

On the last page of your preliminary questionnaire, collect the following information:

Sex   M F Age Group: ___ 17-25   ____ 26-34   ____ 35-44   ____ Over 45

Major: ___ Fine Arts   ____ Humanities   ____ Social Sciences
       ____ Natural Sciences ____ Business   ____ Undecided

Minor: ___ Fine Arts   ___ Humanities   ____ Social Sciences
       ____ Natural Sciences ____ Business   ____ Undecided

# of Hours Completed in Major:_____ # of Hours Completed in Minor _____

If a declared Major, when did you decide?
_____ Before beginning College   ___ Freshman   ___ Sophomore
                               ___ Junior   ___ Senior

How involved do you feel you are in your Major?

___ Seeking a career in this field ___ Enjoy studying but will do another career

___ Interested but not committed ___ Chose major because of other reasons

If Undecided, what areas interest you? (Check all that apply)

___ Fine Arts ___ Humanities ____ Social Sciences ___ Natural Sciences

# of College Credits Completed: _____

AOT ITEM RESPONSE RECORD SHEET

ID #:_____   Group: _____

ITEM #	ANS.	ITEM #	ANS.	ITEM #	ANS.
1		21		41	
2		22		42	
3		23		43	
4		24		44	
5		25		45	
6		26		46	
7		27		47	
8		28		48	
9		29		49	
10		30		50	
11		31		51	
12		32		52	
13		33		53	
14		34		54	
15		35		55	
16		36		56	
17		37		57	
18		38		58	
19		39		59	
20		40		60	

AOT ITEM SELECTION WORKSHEET   PAGE 1

% = the % of people in the group, not of # of items (the # in the groups would be different for each category and for the general group). Be sure to include the sign (+ or -) associated with the difference (delta or "Δ").

Item	Fine Arts "True" Responses			Humanities "True" Responses			Natural Science "True" Responses			Social Sciences "True" Responses			Students-in-General "True" Responses	
	No.	%	Δ	No.	%	Δ	No.	%	Δ	No.	%	Δ	No.	%
01														
02														
03														
04														
05														
06														
07														
08														
09														
10														
11														
12														
13														
14														
15														

AOT ITEM SELECTION WORKSHEET   PAGE 2

% = the % of people in the group, not of # of items (the # in the groups would be different for each category and for the general group). Be sure to include the sign (+ or -) associated with the difference (delta or "Δ").

Item	Fine Arts "True" Responses			Humanities "True" Responses			Natural Science "True" Responses			Social Sciences "True" Responses			Students-in-General "True" Responses	
	No.	%	Δ	No.	%	Δ	No.	%	Δ	No.	%	Δ	No.	%
16														
17														
18														
19														
20														
21														
22														
23														
24														
25														
26														
27														
28														
29														
30														

AOT ITEM SELECTION WORKSHEET   PAGE 3

% = the % of people in the group, not of # of items (the # in the groups would be different for each category and for the general group). Be sure to include the sign (+ or -) associated with the difference (delta or "Δ").

Item	Fine Arts "True" Responses			Humanities "True" Responses			Natural Science "True" Responses			Social Sciences "True" Responses			Students-in-General "True" Responses	
	No.	%	Δ	No.	%	Δ	No.	%	Δ	No.	%	Δ	No.	%
31														
32														
33														
34														
35														
36														
37														
38														
39														
40														
41														
42														
43														
44														
45														

AOT ITEM SELECTION WORKSHEET   PAGE 4

% = the % of people in the group, not of # of items (the # in the groups would be different for each category and for the general group). Be sure to include the sign (+ or –) associated with the difference (delta or "Δ").

Item	Fine Arts "True" Responses			Humanities "True" Responses			Natural Science "True" Responses			Social Sciences "True" Responses			Students-in-General "True" Responses	
	No.	%	Δ	No.	%	Δ	No.	%	Δ	No.	%	Δ	No.	%
46														
47														
48														
49														
50														
51														
52														
53														
54														
55														
56														
57														
58														
59														
60														

AOT SCORING KEYS

New Item #	FINE ARTS		HUMANITIES		NATURAL SCIENCES		SOCIAL SCIENCES	
	Orig. Item #	Pred. Dir. (T/ F)	Orig. Item #	Pred. Dir. (T/ F)	Orig. Item #	Pred. Dir. (T/ F)	Orig. Item #	Pred. Dir. (T/ F)
1								
2								
3								
4								
5								
6								
7								
8								
9								
10								

AOT GROUP DATA SHEET

NORM GROUP ID #	F SCORE	H SCORE	N SCORE	S SCORE

AOT PERCENTILE NORMS TABLES

Fine Arts Scale (N = Total Number of Participants)

(1) Score (Highest to lowest possible score)	(2) Total # of Respondents with this Score (Score = # of items marked in same direction as Scoring Key)	(3) Proportion of Respondents Scoring in Predicted Direction (p= Col (2) / N)	(4) Score Percentage (Col (3) * 100)	(5) Cumulative Percentile
10				
9				
8				
7				
6				
5				
4				
3				
2				
1				

Humanities Scale (N = Total Number of Participants)

(1) Score (Highest to lowest possible score)	(2) Total # of Respondents with this Score (Score = # of items marked in same direction as Scoring Key)	(3) Proportion of Respondents Scoring in Predicted Direction (p= Col (2) / N)	(4) Score Percentage (Col (3) * 100)	(5) Cumulative Percentile
10				
9				
8				
7				
6				
5				
4				
3				
2				
1				

AOT PERCENTILE NORMS TABLES

Natural Sciences Scale (N = Total Number of Participants)

(1) Score (Highest to lowest possible score)	(2) Total # of Respondents with this Score (Score = # of items marked in same direction as Scoring Key)	(3) Proportion of Respondents Scoring in Predicted Direction (p= Col (2) / N)	(4) Score Percentage (Col (3) * 100)	(5) Cumulative Percentile
10				
9				
8				
7				
6				
5				
4				
3				
2				
1				

Social Sciences Scale (N = Total Number of Participants)

(1) Score (Highest to lowest possible score)	(2) Total # of Respondents with this Score (Score = # of items marked in same direction as Scoring Key)	(3) Proportion of Respondents Scoring in Predicted Direction (p= Col (2) / N)	(4) Score Percentage (Col (3) * 100)	(5) Cumulative Percentile
10				
9				
8				
7				
6				
5				
4				
3				
2				
1				

EXERCISE 13
REVISION OF A TEST THROUGH ITEM ANALYSES

INTRODUCTION

Due to the fact that the original version of a test is often longer than is optimal for practical use, there may be a need to shorten it while, at the same time, enhancing its effectiveness. In tests of cognitive ability or achievement, items or choices that do not discriminate only serve as filler and can, thus, be eliminated to the overall instrument. In actual practice, proper item analysis is normally computerized and involves both a large group of preliminary questions and a large pilot testing group. Often the "high" and "low" groups are composed of the upper and lower 27% of the pilot sample. Item analyses yield discrimination indices. A discrimination index tells us how good the item is for discriminating between those who do well on the test as a whole and those who do poorly. This exercise will demonstrate three ways to compute a discrimination index. The first of these ways is to compute a difficulty index. The second way is to compare "high" and "low" performers. The third and final way is to correlate each item score with the score on the total test by means of a *phi coefficient*.

In addition to looking at the discrimination values of items, test revision must also look at the discriminative value of alternative answers. In an effective multiple choice question, the correct answer is chosen more often than any of the incorrect alternatives. All of the incorrect alternative answers should be plausible and, therefore, have a relatively equal chance of being chosen if the examinee guesses.

Remembering that in real test revision, the number of both participants and original questions involved are much larger, this exercise uses the same rationale as would be employed in a larger context. It will use both item analysis and response analysis to revise the original test. It assumes that the present version of the GGAT is too long and that the test will be used to predict across the range of possible performance. The latter assumption requires that there will be an equal number of items at each level of difficulty.

MATERIALS NEEDED

All	Copies of the previously-administered GGAT (maximum 40 for exercise)
1	Copy of the GGAT Correct Answers Table (Parts A and B)
1	Copy of the GGAT Total Right Answers Table
1	Copy of the Worksheet for Discrimination Value
1	Copy of the Comparative Procedures Table
1	Copy of the Worksheet for Evaluating Response Alternatives
2	Highlighters (of different color)

✓ If needed, sample data for this exercise that may be used for item analysis can be found in the companion CD-Rom in the data file "*Ex13_GGAT_Data.xls.*"

✓ A second file includes answers for the item analysis exercise for the sample data, entitled "*Ex13-ExampleData_Answers.doc.*"

PROCEDURE

A. DETERMINING DIFFICULTY LEVEL OF QUESTIONS

The difficulty level of an item is defined as the percent of participants who get an item right. If a large percentage of people get an item right, then this indicates that the question was easy. Thus, even though the term used is "difficulty level," this is really a measure of ease. **NOTE**: For students or instructors that do not have sample GGAT data available, data for this exercise that may be used for item analysis can be found in the companion CD-Rom in the data file *"Ex13_GGAT_Data.xls."* If using this data, please skip to Step 4. A second file includes answers for the item analysis exercise for the sample data, entitled *"Ex13-ExampleData_Answers.doc."*

Step 1.   *Select tests for analysis and assign numbers to administered tests.*
The class will randomly select copies of previously-administered GGAT. Choose an approximately equal number of tests from each class member so that the total number chosen does not exceed 40. Then, starting with the number 1, one class member will take as many numbers as needed for his/her tests. The next class member will take the next set of numbers for his/her tests, and so on, until all administered tests are numbered consecutively.

Step 2.   *Chart "right" answers for each item for each participant.*
Each person will record the results from the tests he/she administered in the appropriately numbered rows of the GGAT Correct Answers Table (e.g., if tests are marked 24-28, then use rows 24-28).
a. Put a "1" in the box for an item when the item was answered correctly.
b. Put a "0" in the box for an item when the item was answered incorrectly.
c. Place the number of questions answered correctly (total # of "1"s) in the last column for each row on Part B of the table (column labeled "Total Score").

Step 3.   *Collate data.*
Class members will share their data so that the whole class will have completed copies of the GGAT Correct Answers Table (Parts A and B).

Step 4.   *Select work groups and divide the questions.*
The class will divide into five workgroups. Each group will assume responsibility for six items of the GGAT.

Step 5. *Calculate the proportion correct for each item for each group.*
Using the "Original Item Order" section of the GGAT Total Right
Answers Table, each group will complete the rows connected to their
assigned items. This involves:
a. counting the number of people who had the right answer and putting
the total in the "# of Participants with Right Answer" column.
b. calculating the proportion of people getting the right answer (difficulty
level) and putting that number in the "Proportion with Right Answer."
The formula for this calculation is the total number of people who got
the question right (from Step 5, Part a) divided by the total number of
people who took the test (e.g., 40).

Step 6. *Create a unified list of questions in order of difficulty.*
a. Each group will share their data so that the rest of the class will have
complete copies of the "Original Item Order" section of the GGAT
Total Right Answers Table.
b. Once this section is complete, each student will reorder the items in
order of difficulty using the "In Order of Difficulty" section of the
GGAT Total Right Answers Table, so that the easiest items are at the
top of the table and most difficult items are at the bottom of the table.
The column "Proportion with Correct Answer" is completed by
copying difficulty level from the original item order section.

Step 7. *Select questions.*
On the "In Order of Item Difficulty" section of the GGAT Total Right
Answers Table, the class will choose questions by putting an "X" in the
"Good Item?" column next to each question selected. The number of
questions selected should be approximately 80% of the original number of
items (for the GGAT, this would be 24 items selected). The criteria for
choosing should be the following steps:
a. First, select all questions with difficulty levels (proportions right)
between .25 and .75 (i.e., eliminating questions that are too easy or too
difficult and keeping questions that maximize discrimination).
b. If this does not yield sufficient questions to meet the 80% criteria,
move to the boundaries of .20 and .80.
c. If this does not yield sufficient questions to meet the 80% criteria,
continue extending the boundaries by increments of .05 or less at both
ends until there are a sufficient number of questions.

Step 8. *Record the results.*
On the Comparative Procedures Table, place an "X" in the "Difficulty
Level" column for each question selected in Step 7.

B. **DETERMINING DISCRIMINATION VALUE OF QUESTIONS BY THE USE OF DIFFERENCE SCORES**

Step 1.   *Rank total scores.*

Using the GGAT Correct Answers Table (Part B), examine the "Total Score" column and rank all scores from highest to lowest. The number "1" will indicate the highest score. Place the rank just outside the column for "Total Score" on Part B of the GGAT Correct Answers Table.

Step 2.   *Create High and Low Groups.*

On the GGAT Correct Answers Table, highlight the rows containing the overall highest 10 test scores in the same color (these scores comprise the High Group). Then, using a different color, highlight the rows containing the lowest 10 test scores (the scores comprise the Low Group).

Step 3.   *Form work groups.*

The class will form into the same five workgroups as in Part A, Step 4 and assume responsibility for the same six items of the GGAT.

Step 4.   *Compute the differences between High and Low Groups (D).*

The work groups formed in Step 4 will, on the Worksheet for Discrimination Values, record the following information on the appropriately numbered rows for each of their six items:

a. Determine the number of people in the High Group who answered each of the six items correctly and record this in column (2) "# Right High" on the Worksheet for Discrimination Values.

b. Determine the number of people in the Low Group who answered each of the six items correctly and record this in column (3) "# Right Low" on the Worksheet for Discrimination Values.

c. On the Worksheet, calculate the Difference Value by subtracting the number in column 3 from the number in column 2. Record this Difference Value in column 4.

Step 5.   *Collate the data.*

Groups will share their data so that the rest of the class may complete the "Difference Value" section of the Worksheet for Discrimination Value.

Step 6.   *Select questions.*

The class will choose 24 items from the GGAT (80% of the original test) that have the highest difference values (D) in column 4 of the Worksheet. Mark these items with an "X" in the "Good Item?" column of "Difference Value" section of the Worksheet.

Step 7.   *Record the results.*

On the Comparative Procedures Table, place an "X" in the "Difference Value" column for each question selected in Step 6.

C.   DETERMINING DISCRIMINATION VALUE OF QUESTIONS BY THE USE OF
      ITEM CORRELATION

Step 1.   *Compute value for dividing participants into two groups.*
                 Using the "Total Score" number on the GGAT Correct Answers Table and
                 the ranks information (computed in Part B, Step 1), calculate the median
                 of the total scores so that all the tests will be evenly divided into two
                 groups. Those test scores above the median will be called the "Top"
                 group and those below the median will be the "Bottom" group.

Step 2.   *Form work groups.*
                 The class will re-form into the same five workgroups as in Part B, Step 3
                 and assume responsibility for the same six items of the GGAT.

Step 3.   *Measure the relationship between each item and the Total Score.*
                 For each item, the work group will compute the relationship between the
                 number of participants that get an item correct (the total at the bottom of
                 each column on the GGAT Correct Answers Table) and their Grand Total
                 Score (the last column on Part B of the GGAT Correct Answers Table).
                 For a given item,:
                 a.   determine how many people got that question right and had a
                       Grand Total Score that was above the median (were in the "Top"
                       Group). Record this number in Column "A" of the "Phi
                       Coefficient" section on the Worksheet for Discrimination Values
                       (this will be the number "A" in the phi formula).
                 b.   determine how many people got that question wrong and had a
                       Grand Total Score that was above the median (were in the "Top"
                       Group). Record this number in Column "B" of the "Phi
                       Coefficient" section on the Worksheet for Discrimination Values
                       (this will be the number "B" in the phi formula).
                 c.   determine how many people got that question right and had a
                       Grand Total Score that was below the median (were in the
                       "Bottom" Group). Record this number in Column "C" of the "Phi
                       Coefficient" section on the Worksheet for Discrimination Values
                       (this will be the number "C" in the phi formula).
                 d.   determine how many people got that question wrong and had a
                       Grand Total Score that was below the median (were in the
                       "Bottom" Group). Record this number in Column "D" of the "Phi
                       Coefficient" section on the Worksheet for Discrimination Values
                       (this will be the number "D" in the phi formula).

e. use the following phi coefficient formula to calculate *phi*:

Cell Values:
A = # in the Top Group answering correctly
B = # in the Top Group answering incorrectly
C = # in the Low Group answering correctly
D = # in the Low Group answering incorrectly

Formula for *phi*: $\phi = \dfrac{(AD - BC)}{\sqrt{(A+B)(C+D)(A+C)(B+D)}}$

Record these phi values in the "Phi" column of the "Phi Coefficient" section on the Worksheet for Discrimination Values.

Step 4. *Collate data.*
Groups will share their data so that the rest of the class may complete the "Phi Coefficient" section of the Worksheet for Discrimination Value.

Step 5. *Select questions.*
The class will choose 24 items from the GGAT (80% of the original test) that have the highest positive phi values in the "phi" column of the Worksheet. Mark these items with an "X" in the "Good Item?" column of "Phi Coefficient" section of the Worksheet.

Step 6. *Record the results.*
On the Comparative Procedures Table, place an "X" in the "Phi Coefficient" column for each question selected in Step 5.

Step 7. *Complete the "Number of Times Chosen" column.*
In the last column of the Comparative Procedures Table, add the total number of times (0-3) that a given item was selected for use in the final version of the test.

D. EVALUATING ALTERNATIVES
NOTE: To save time, this portion of the exercise will be performed on a set of previously collected responses to the GGAT. If desired, students can also perform the same analyses on their own GGAT data by recording all responses to the 40 questions on the GGAT.

Step 1. *Form work groups.*
The class will re-form into the same five workgroups as in Part C, Step 2 and assume responsibility for the same six items of the GGAT.

Step 2. *Calculate expected alternative responses.*
For each item, the work group will use the data on the Worksheet for Evaluating Response Alternatives to calculate the number of people expected to choose each alternative answer choices. Ideally, all those who incorrectly responded to an item would choose (or guess) evenly and randomly among the alternative choices.
a. Add the number of people who answered the item incorrectly.

      b. Divide this number by the number of incorrect answer choices (for the GGAT this will always be three).

      c. Record this number of expected responses in the "Expected" column of the Worksheet for Evaluating Response Alternatives.

Step 3.   *Collate data.*
Groups will then share their data with the class so everyone has a complete copy of the Worksheet for Evaluating Response Alternatives.

Step 4.   *Choose question numbers for rewriting.*
      a. Using the Worksheet for Evaluating Response Alternatives, decide which items responses need to be revised to meet the following two criteria:

        (1) The correct answer is chosen more often than any incorrect alternative.

        (2) Those who incorrectly responded to a given item choice (approximately) equally among the alternative choices.

      b. If the class feels an item's responses need to be rewritten, write an "X" in the "Rewrite?" column on the Worksheet for Evaluating Response Alternatives.

      c. Rewrite any bad questions by revising those alternatives that are too high or too low in plausibility. The group's best judgment should determine what kind of change would make an alternative more or less plausible.

QUESTIONS

1. Looking at the Comparative Procedures Table, answer the following:
    a.   What were the differences in the item lists chosen by each method?
    b.   How many questions made it to the final version in all three methods? Did you have enough that were chosen by all three to meet the criterion of selecting 80% of the items from the original test (24 items for the GGAT)? If not, did using those selected by two out of three methods enable you to reach criterion?

2. What does a negative difference value or phi coefficient tell you? What is the reasoning behind eliminating items with negative differences or phi coefficients?

3. Why is it undesirable to have an alternative that is so implausible that none of the participants select it? How does this affect how the participants answer the question?

GGAT CORRECT ANSWERS TABLE: PART A

Test	Item 1	Item 2	Item 3	Item 4	Item 5	Item 6	Item 7	Item 8	Item 9	Item 10	Item 11	Item 12	Item 13	Item 14	Item 15
1															
2															
3															
4															
5															
6															
7															
8															
9															
10															
11															
12															
13															
14															
15															
16															
17															
18															
19															
20															
21															
22															
23															
24															
25															
26															
27															
28															
28															
30															
31															
32															
33															
34															
35															
36															
37															
38															
39															
40															
# Right															

GGAT CORRECT ANSWERS TABLE: PART B

Test	Item 16	Item 17	Item 18	Item 19	Item 20	Item 21	Item 22	Item 23	Item 24	Item 25	Item 26	Item 27	Item 29	Item 30	Item 31	Total Score
1																
2																
3																
4																
5																
6																
7																
8																
9																
10																
11																
12																
13																
14																
15																
16																
17																
18																
19																
20																
21																
22																
23																
24																
25																
26																
27																
28																
28																
30																
31																
32																
33																
34																
35																
36																
37																
38																
39																
40																
# Right																

233

GGAT TOTAL RIGHT ANSWERS TABLE

	Original Item Order			In Order of Item Difficulty		
Item #	# of Tests with Correct Answer	Proportion with Correct Answer		Item #	Proportion with Correct Answer	Good Item?
1						
2						
3						
4						
5						
6						
7						
8						
9						
10						
11						
12						
13						
14						
15						
16						
17						
18						
19						
20						
21						
22						
23						
24						
25						
26						
27						
28						
29						
30						

WORKSHEET FOR DISCRIMINATION VALUES

DIFFERENCE VALUE					PHI COEFFICIENT					
(1) Item #	(2) # Right High	(3) # Right Low	(4) Diff. = (2)-(3)	Good Item?	A	B	C	D	Phi	Good Item?
1										
2										
3										
4										
5										
6										
7										
8										
9										
10										
11										
12										
13										
14										
15										
16										
17										
18										
19										
20										
21										
22										
23										
24										
25										
26										
27										
28										
29										
30										

COMPARATIVE PROCEDURES TABLE

Item #	Difficulty Level	Difference Value	Phi Coefficient	Total Times Chosen
1				
2				
3				
4				
5				
6				
7				
8				
9				
10				
11				
12				
13				
14				
15				
16				
17				
18				
19				
20				
21				
22				
23				
24				
25				
26				
27				
28				
29				
30				

WORKSHEET FOR EVALUATING RESPONSE ALTERNATIVES

Item #	Response A	Response B	Response C	Response D	# Expected	Rewrite?
1	4	7	*29*	0		
2	7	6	*24*	3		
3	6	*20*	12	2		
4	5	2	*27*	6		
5	2	3	*32*	3		
6	*29*	1	8	2		
7	0	*36*	0	4		
8	19	2	1	*18*		
9	3	0	*31*	6		
10	*31*	3	6	0		
11	6	16	*10*	8		
12	4	3	*25*	8		
13	1	*38*	1	0		
14	0	0	0	*40*		
15	0	*40*	0	0		
16	10	10	*11*	9		
17	9	*23*	7	1		
18	*40*	0	0	0		
19	1	*37*	2	0		
20	0	1	0	*39*		
21	25	*9*	1	5		
22	4	8	*24*	4		
23	3	*36*	1	0		
24	*37*	3	0	0		
25	0	0	*32*	8		
26	18	*17*	3	2		
27	0	1	*38*	1		
28	11	5	*23*	1		
29	8	21	*6*	5		
30	2	4	*28*	6		

EXERCISE 14
BUILDING A FAKING SCALE:
THE SOCIAL DESIRABILITY RESPONSE SCALE (SDR)

INTRODUCTION

Sometime called a "social desirability" or "lie" scale, this assessment tool by design identifies patterns of extreme responses to personality measures. Specifically, this type of scale is designed to identify respondents whose pattern of responses on a personality measure is in the extremely "positive" end of the continuum. This is a controversial area of assessment because there are many motivating and individual-difference factors to possibly explain why a person rates him-/herself consistently more "positively" on select characteristics both within and across personality dimensions.

The argument for this assessment is to attempt to identify examinees presenting an overly positive representation of themselves for a specific purpose (e.g., to get hired into a desired job position). The key to identifying this type of examinee, in comparison to other types of examinees completing the same personality measure, is through the design of the personality test itself (instructions, content of response items) and also the inclusion of a follow-up assessment in response to the initial personality testing scores.

This exercise demonstrates several stages in the development of a social desirability test (faking scale) covering aspects of personality testing in psychology. The Social Desirability Response (SDR) Scale will be used as an example of how to assess social desirability response tendencies among individuals in a testing situation, having applicability toward testing issues in research, education, and the workplace.

MATERIALS NEEDED

1	Copy of the Informed Consent Form Template (Appendix A)
2	Copies of the Universal Demographic Sheet (Appendix B)
1	Copy of the SDR Tips for Writing Likert (5-point) Scale Items
1-2	Copies of the following materials:
	Study guides for Social and Personality Psychology textbooks
	Psychology of Personality textbooks
	Social Psychology textbooks
1+	Copies of the SDR Group Data Sheet (data for 16 class members)
1	Copy of the SDR Statistical Summary Sheet
1	Copy of the Computation of Student's *t* (Appendix D)
1	Copy of Significance Table for *t-test* (from a Statistics text)

PROCEDURE

A.   TEST PREPARATION

   Step 1.   *State the purpose of the test.*

   Ordinarily, the class should reach a consensus about the desired purpose of this test. In this exercise, the purpose of the test will be to test college students' social desirability (faking) response tendencies in a testing situation. Knowledge from this exercise may assist in the development of reliable and validity measures as "screening" device, as part of a larger test battery, in different testing contexts (e.g., work, school).

Step 2.   *Item selection and writing.*
   a.   Class will form groups of three or four people. Each group will develop items using the following information references for content:
        (1)   Study guides for Social and Personality Psychology textbooks,
        (2)   Psychology of Personality textbooks, and/or
        (3)   Social Psychology textbooks.
   b.   Each group will write 30 test items using the SDR Tips for Writing Likert Scale Questions sheet as a reference.

Step 3.   *Write test items and construct scale.*
Each group should review the SDR Tips for Writing Likert (five-point) Scale Items sheet before beginning item writing. Each group will produce a list of 30 Likert scale items, in the following format:

   a.   At the top of each test page, present the Likert scale for each list of questions:

1	2	3	4	5
Highly Unlike Me	Somewhat Unlike Me	Neutral	Somewhat Like Me	Highly Like Me

   b.   Write items to be either "I always…." or "I never…" statements. Each of the items should refer to prosocial, positive attributes in personality and social behavior. The following is the basic item structure, with a space for the Likert scale response number (corresponds to Likert scale at the top of each test page):

        (Item #) ____. (Item stem)_____.   ____

Example item:
        15.   I always agree with what my instructor tells me.   __4__

   c.   These lists should be typed with single spacing within the test item and triple spacing in between items so that they may be cut apart.

Step 4.   *Create test instructions that precede test items.*
The test examinee is to be instructed to respond to each statement, judging how much the statement reflects who the examinee is on a regular basis (e.g., daily). This Likert scale rating will be put in the response space next to each item statement.

Step 5.   *Create necessary additional test administration materials for the SDR.*
              The class will form three work groups.

    a.   One group will also create and type up an Informed Consent Form (Appendix A). This group will also be responsible for making copies of the Universal Demographic Sheet (Appendix B).

    b.   Another group will create one set of instructions for the test taker and another set for the test administrator.

    c.   A third group will take the lists of items and:
        (1)   neatly cut the test items into strips,
        (2)   arrange the test item strips in random order on pieces of paper, so that they can be photocopied as test forms; and
        (3)   number the test items on the line preceding the item stem.
               Note: Ensure that a Likert scale is at the top of each page for each test form.

    d.   Develop a scoring plan for social desirability (faking). Specifically, scoring will identify high "faking" behavior as being potentially indicated by a pattern of extremely high self-ratings on the SDR scale across 30 items. On a five-point Likert scale, a person whom consistently chooses the most "socially desirable" self-rating option would be scored as being high on SDR or "faking" tendency. Group members need to "brainstorm" the range of scores for the categories of "high," "moderate" and "low" SDR (faking) tendency.

B.   ADMINISTRATION

Step 1.   *Producing the preliminary version of the SDR.*

    a.   The class will design a first page for the test, with the following items:
        (1)   ID #,
        (2)   Relevant information chosen in *Step 5a*, and
        (3)   Instructions for the examinee created in *Step 5b*.

    b.   The next pages are photocopies of the pages created in *Step 5c* ((1)-(3)).

    c.   The last page is a copy of the scoring plan created in *Step 5d*.

Step 2.   *Make sufficient copies.*

    a.   Each class member will make a copy of the scoring plan for his/her own use.

    b.   Each class member will make two copies of the Informed Consent Form, Universal Demographic Sheet, and completed SDR test for administration.

Step 3.　　　*Administering the preliminary version of the SDR.*
Each class member should administer the test to two people (one male, one female) with at least a H.S. degree and 18 years of age or older. The student testing may be done individually or in a group. Information regarding gender will be collected on the Universal Demographic Sheet.

Step. 4.　　　*Record results.*
a.　　Class members will use the created scoring plan to score the tests they administered (i.e., low, moderate, or high SDR (faking) scores).
b.　　Each class member will use the first lines of the appropriate section of the SDR Group Data Sheets to record each participant's information and scores that includes columns for the demographic items selected as relevant.

C.　　ANALYSIS
Step 1.　　　*Collate the data.*
Class members will share their data so that every person will have a completed copy of the SDR Group Data Sheet.

Step 2.　　　*Compute descriptive statistics.*
a.　　Each student should compute the Mean and Standard Deviation for:
(1)　　Men only.
(2)　　Women only.
(3)　　The whole group.
b.　　Transfer the results to the SDR Statistical Summary Sheet.

Step 3.　　　*Compute the difference statistic.*
a.　　Using the data from the male and female groups, each class member will compute an independent group's *t* test (Appendix D) to investigate the significance of the difference between the SDR scores.
b.　　Using a Table of Significance for *t*, class members will determine the *p* value of the obtained *t* value (area in tail).
c.　　Transfer the results to the SDR Statistical Summary Sheet.

QUESTIONS
1.　　How does this test differ from tests like the Projective Personality Test (PPT)? How is it similar?

2.　　Would you expect the scores on the SDR to change or remain stable over time? Why or why not?

3.　　What do these results suggest to you about gender differences in testing-related faking behavior?

SDR TIPS FOR WRITING LIKERT (5-POINT) SCALE ITEMS

1.   Each question should contain only one main idea in the self-statement to be responded to by the examinee.

2.   Items should be expressed in precise language.

3.   Avoid irrelevant sources of difficulty in the stem (e.g., difficult vocabulary and jargon).

4.   Use negatively worded items sparingly and when you do, set off the negative aspect by underlining or capitalizing the word that indicates negation (e.g., not, NOT).

5.   To assess the extreme responses, use words such as *always and never* in these self-statements.

SDR GROUP DATA SHEET

Male		Female	
ID #	SDR Score	ID #	SDR Score

SDR STATISTICAL SUMMARY SHEET

<u>Male</u> Statistics:

    Mean of SDR Scores _____

    S.D. of SDR Scores _____

<u>Female</u> Statistics:

    Mean of SDR Scores _____

    S.D. of SDR Scores _____

<u>Whole Group</u> Statistics:

    Mean of SDR Scores _____

    S.D. of SDR Scores _____

Difference Statistic between Men and Women:

    $t =$ _____

    $p =$ _____

EXERCISE 15
PREDICTIVE VALIDITY

INTRODUCTION

Predictive validity refers to the extent to which a predictor item is able to predict performance on a criterion task that is measured at a later time. The result of studying predictive validity is a set of decisions regarding cut-off points for determining success or failure. Depending on where the cut-off is set, these decisions may be more or less accurate.

Using a case study, this exercise will investigate the predictive validity of two different tests for selecting applicants to a university. Students will compute correlations between each test (predictor) and a later GPA (criterion performance), prepare expectancy tables to summarize the relationship, and create a scatterplot to represent it graphically. You will set up various cut-off scores to examine different types of decision regarding admission and the extent of any errors incurred by basing admission on tests such as these.

MATERIALS NEEDED

1	Copy of the ABC College Case Study
1	Copy of the Correlation Data Between CAT and GPA Sheet (two pages)
1	Copy of the Correlation Data Between WAT and GPA Sheet (two pages)
1	Copy of the Significance of r Table (any statistics text)
1	Copy of the Scatterplot and Scattergram Templates for CAT and GPA
1	Copy of the Expectancy Table Templates for CAT (two tables)
1	Copy of the Scatterplot and Scattergram Templates for WAT and GPA
1	Copy of the Expectancy Table Templates (two tables) for WAT

✓ If needed, two datasets for statistical analyses are available on the accompanying CD-Rom (*Ex15-CAT_Data.xls*, *Ex15-WAT_Data.xls*).

PROCEDURE

Step 1. *Read the case study.*
Each class member will read the ABC College Case Study and review the corresponding correlation data sheets from the predictive study examining the relationships among CAT, WAT, and GPA (e.g., Correlation Data Between CAT and GPA: Part A).

Step 2. *Decide on balance of prediction errors (decision points).*
The class should discuss the implications of cut-offs and decision-making. Due to the fact that we know there will be error (variation) in any test, decide whether your cut-off should be more attuned to avoiding false positives (i.e., succeeds on predictor [test] but does not succeed on criterion performance [GPA]), or false negatives (i.e., does not succeed on predictor [test] but succeeds on the criterion performance [GPA]).

Step 3. *Form work groups.*

The class members will form two work groups. One group will complete *Steps 4 - 10* using the data from the College Aptitude Test (CAT), while the other group will complete *Steps 4 - 10* using the data from the World Affairs Test (WAT).

Step 4. *Calculate measures of central tendency and variability (dispersion).*

Using the data provided on the correlation data sheets (e.g., Correlation Data Between CAT and GPA: Part A), compute the mean and standard deviation for both the predictor (either CAT or WAT) scores and for the criterion (GPA) performance. Write your answers at the bottom of Page 2 of the appropriate Correlation Data sheet.

Step 5. *Calculate correlation coefficients between the test score and the GPA.*

a.   Calculate a validity coefficient (correlation coefficient) between the assigned test and GPA, and record the value on the appropriate Correlation Data Sheet.

b.   Look up the obtained r in a Table of Significance, and record the p value on the appropriate Correlation Data Sheet.

c.   Calculate the effect size (r^2), and record the value on the appropriate Correlation Data Sheet.

d.   An alternative to doing steps 5.a. through 5.c. is to do the calculations using Excel or SPSS. Based on pilot testing with past lab students, data files have been created for this purpose. The data file for the CAT is entitled "*Ex15-CAT_Data.xls*" and the data file for the WAT is entitled "*Ex15-WAT_Data.xls*." These data files are provided on the accompanying lab manual CD-Rom.

Step 6. *Prepare scattergram.*

a.   Using the provided Scattergram template, draw a " / " mark in the appropriate box where the test scores and GPA intersect for each of participants in the Correlation Data Tables. There will be a total of 40 "/ " marks.

b.   Count the number of "/" marks in each box, and write this total in the upper left hand corner of the box.

c.   For each score level, add the total # of students in that column. Record this number in the last row.

Step 7. *Prepare scatterplot.*

a.   Using the data from the appropriate Correlation Data sheet and the provided Scatterplot template, place a dot at the intersection of each participant's pair (i.e., test score and GPA) of scores. There will be 40 dots.

b.   Draw a line through the dots. The angle of this line is a judgement based on your decision about which angle would make the line come closest to the most number of dots (i.e., a "line-of-best-fit").

c.   Graphing the scatterplot can also be done in either Excel or SPSS with the electronic data files provided.

Step 8.   *Convert frequencies to proportions.*
In order to predict the GPA from the CAT or the WAT, you need to see how many participants at different levels of test score obtained different later GPAs. To get this data, divide the number of participants obtaining a particular combination of Score and GPA by the total number of students at that score level (see last row of scattergram). You should have six different sets of proportions (six columns) and seven proportions (seven rows) in each set. Write these proportions in parentheses in each box of the scattergram.

Step 9.   *Create the expectancy table.*
Copy the proportions obtained in *Step 8* to the corresponding boxes in the appropriate Expectancy Table. This box will allow you to estimate the range of GPA that a person is likely to earn given his or her test score.

Step 10.   *Create cut-off point for criterion.*
a.   Due to the fact that a GPA of less than 2.0 puts a student on probation, this seems an appropriate criterion cut-off for "Succeed" and "Not Succeed." On the Expectancy Table, a double line is drawn across the table (horizontally) at the bottom of the 2.0 to 2.4 interval.
b.   Complete the Success Expectancy Table. This table will consolidate and simplify the information in the Expectancy Table. The Success Expectancy Table has only two rows. The top row contains all people who had a "successful" GPA (i.e., 2.0 or better) while the bottom row contains all people who failed on the criterion (i.e., GPA lower than 2.0). The six columns represent the six interval ranges on the predictor test. From the Expectancy Table, add all the proportions above and below your cut-off line within each predictor score interval. Put these sums in the appropriate boxes of the Success Expectancy Table. The Success Expectancy Table will then tell you the probability of succeeding or failing on the criterion performance (GPA) for a given range of predictor (CAT or WAT) scores.

Step 11.   *Create cut-off point for test score.*
Selecting a cut-off point for the test scores requires some trial and error. The object is to select the score that will accurately pick the highest proportions of both Succeeds and Not Succeeds, while minimizing both false positives and false negatives. To do this, you must do the following.
a.   Use a pencil to draw a tentative cut-off line vertically at the beginning of a test score interval on the Success Expectancy Table created in *Step 10*.

b.   Compute the number of "hits," or *true positives* and *true negatives*. These are the people for whom the test made a correct prediction. Based on their exceeding the cut-off score, the test predicted that they would succeed and they did (true positive), or, based on their not exceeding the cut-off score, the test predicted they would fail and they did (true negative).

c.   Compute the number of "misses," or *false positives* and *false negatives*. These are the people for whom the test made a incorrect prediction. For these people, based on their exceeding the cut-off score, the test predicted they would succeed and they did not (false positive), or, based on their not exceeding the cut-off score, the test predicted they would fail and they did not (false negative).

d.   Repeat this procedure at other potential cut-off points until you feel you have reached the optimum balance point based on criteria decided upon by class discussion in *Step 2*. That will be your cut-off score for the predictor test. Place a vertical double line in ink at that point on the Success Expectancy chart.

Step 12.   *Compare results.*
Each of the two work groups will write on the blackboard the following results from their work:

a.   The validity coefficient, its significance level, and effect size.

b.   The test cut-off score and the percentage of hits, the percentage of false positives, and the percentage of false negatives related to that cut-off score.

These pieces of data will allow you to decide which test is the better instrument to use as a predictor in selecting admission candidates.

QUESTIONS

1. Are the obtained validity coefficients of the CAT and the WAT significant? What does this information indicate concerning the overall predictive validity of the test scores?

2. What could be done in test development to raise the rate of "true positives" (accuracy in prediction, in which future good performers are selected) and "true negatives" (accuracy in prediction, in which future bad performers are rejected)?

3. What could be done in test development to reduce the rate of "false positives" (inaccuracy in prediction, in which future bad performers are selected) and "false negatives" (inaccuracy in prediction, in which future good performers are rejected)?

ABC COLLEGE CASE STUDY

The ABC college is a small school that draws the majority of its students from the college preparatory program of the local high school. Up until now, selection of students has relied solely on high school grades and recommendations from teachers. The college wants to require that in applying for admission, students take its own College Aptitude Test and World Affairs Test in addition to taking the ACT. The "College Aptitude Test" is a test of verbal comprehension, quantitative reasoning, and abstract thinking. The "World Affairs Test" covers knowledge of current events, political affairs, cultural and sports activities, and general information in recent history.

The college is aware of the fact that practical considerations often lead to the premature use of test scores before they have been properly validated for selection. A test with good predictive validity may legitimately be used for selection purposes. Due to the fact that the college admissions counselors are conscientious about trying to use valid methods for deciding admissions, they decide to study the predictive validity of their proposed admission tests. Predictive validity requires correlating a test performance with a criterion performance that occurs later in time. To do their study, they administered the two tests and the ACT to all forty individuals enrolled in the college preparatory program early in their senior year. The criterion measure the college chose was student GPA at the end of the first full year of college. They chose this measure while acknowledging that such a measure, taken at one point in time, is limited in its reliability and represents a limited range of academic performance. They also recognize that the results of this study should be cross-validated on another comparable sample of participants before it is actually used.

In order to ensure that the test results were not used by university officials in making decisions about whom to select for admission or in assigning grades in individual courses, the results were "locked up" and were not available to anyone selecting or counseling students, or to any faculty members in the courses taken by freshmen. By doing so, the ABC College felt this study would provide a clear examination of the usefulness of the tests over and above their current method of selection. This procedure would also reduce the chances that the criterion (GPA) might be artificially related to or "contaminated" by, knowledge of a person's test score.

The College proposed to create cut-off scores for each of the tests to use as a factor in deciding whether or not to admit. A GPA of less than 2.0 puts a student on probation and, if they continue to perform this way they will not graduate. We might say that these students have been "unsuccessful" (at least thus far in their academic careers). Therefore, a GPA of 2.0 will be used as the criterion cut-off score. The aim is to establish cut-off scores for the test (predictor) that will best predict success (above cut-off) on the criterion score. The cut-off score chosen must be one that maximizes the probability of choosing people who succeed (stay at or above 2.0), and not choosing those who will not. The other criterion is that such a cut-off would minimize the probabilities of either choosing people for admission who will not succeed in college (false positives) or not admitting people who might have succeeded (false negatives).

Even after cut-off scores are established, the college officials intend to use additional information about applicants gathered by interviews, application blanks, and letters of recommendation as resources for admission decisions. They know that, even under the best conditions, predictions about academic success are not always accurate since many unknown and changing factors in both the individual and the school environment preclude error-free prediction. The correlation data sheets provided here present the data from the students in their predictive study.

CORRELATION DATA BETWEEN CAT AND GPA: PART A
(PREDICTIVE STUDY PARTICIPANTS #s 1-20)

ID	x (CAT Test)	y (GPA)	xy	x^2	y^2
1	618	3.9			
2	627	3.9			
3	625	3.7			
4	681	3.6			
5	614	3.3			
6	646	3.1			
7	396	3.0			
8	451	3.0			
9	598	2.9			
10	595	2.9			
11	336	2.7			
12	595	2.7			
13	528	2.2			
14	785	2.6			
15	405	2.6			
16	548	2.5			
17	600	2.5			
18	630	2.0			
19	493	2.3			
20	590	2.2			

CORRELATION DATA BETWEEN CAT AND GPA: PART B
(PREDICTIVE STUDY PARTICIPANTS #s 21-40)

ID	x (CAT Test)	y (GPA)	xy	x^2	y^2
21	491	2.2			
22	540	2.0			
23	558	2.0			
24	601	2.0			
25	481	1.7			
26	459	1.7			
27	592	1.7			
28	505	1.7			
29	456	1.7			
30	543	1.5			
31	438	1.5			
32	431	1.5			
33	570	1.4			
34	206	1.4			
35	360	1.4			
36	623	1.4			
37	512	1.3			
38	574	1.3			
39	496	0.9			
40	381	0.9			
$n = 40$	$\Sigma x =$	$\Sigma y =$	$\Sigma xy =$	$\Sigma x^2 =$	$\Sigma y^2 =$

$$M_x = \frac{\Sigma X}{n} = \qquad\qquad SD_x = \sqrt{\frac{\Sigma(X - M_x)^2}{n-1}} =$$

$$r = \frac{(n\Sigma xy) - (\Sigma x \Sigma y)}{\sqrt{\left[n\Sigma x^2 - (\Sigma x)^2\right]\left[n\Sigma y^2 - (\Sigma y)^2\right]}} =$$

$$p = \qquad\qquad\qquad\qquad\qquad r^2 =$$

CORRELATION DATA BETWEEN WAT AND GPA: PART A
(PREDICTIVE STUDY PARTICIPANTS #s 1-20)

ID	x (WAT Test)	y (GPA)	xy	x^2	y^2
1	76	3.9			
2	36	3.9			
3	37	3.7			
4	42	3.6			
5	47	3.3			
6	24	3.1			
7	51	3.0			
8	57	3.0			
9	49	2.9			
10	29	2.9			
11	55	2.7			
12	42	2.7			
13	62	2.2			
14	59	2.6			
15	41	2.6			
16	38	2.5			
17	37	2.5			
18	75	2.0			
19	46	2.3			
20	71	2.2			

CORRELATION DATA BETWEEN WAT AND GPA: PART B
(PREDICTIVE STUDY PARTICIPANTS #s 21-40)

ID	x (WAT Test)	y (GPA)	xy	x^2	y^2
21	51	2.2			
22	73	2.0			
23	67	2.0			
24	49	2.0			
25	64	1.7			
26	62	1.7			
27	57	1.7			
28	54	1.7			
29	45	1.7			
30	55	1.5			
31	50	1.5			
32	53	1.5			
33	61	1.4			
34	42	1.4			
35	39	1.4			
36	35	1.4			
37	38	1.3			
38	38	1.3			
39	37	0.9			
40	41	0.9			
$n = 40$	$\Sigma x =$	$\Sigma y =$	$\Sigma xy =$	$\Sigma x^2 =$	$\Sigma y^2 =$

$$M_x = \frac{\Sigma X}{n} = \qquad\qquad SD_x = \sqrt{\frac{\Sigma (X - M_x)^2}{n-1}} =$$

$$r = \frac{(n\Sigma xy) - (\Sigma x \Sigma y)}{\sqrt{\left[n\Sigma x^2 - (\Sigma x)^2\right]\left[n\Sigma y^2 - (\Sigma y)^2\right]}} =$$

$$p = \qquad\qquad\qquad\qquad\qquad r^2 =$$

SCATTERGRAM FOR CAT AND GPA

	CAT SCORES					
3.5- +						
3.0-3.4						
2.5-2.9						
2.0-2.4						
GPA 1.5-1.9						
1.0-1.4						
< 1.0						
	Less than 300	300-399	400-499	500-599	600-699	700 +

Total # of Score
Level   N=   N=   N=   N=   N=   N=

SCATTER PLOT SHOWING RELATIONSHIP OF CAT SCORES AND GPA

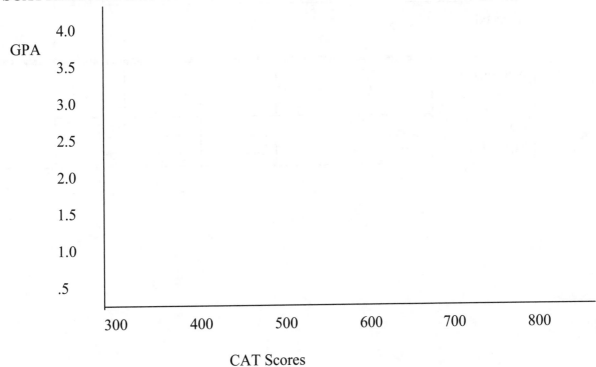

CAT Scores

EXPECTANCY TABLE FOR CAT AND GPA

GPA	Less than 300	300-399	400-499	500-599	600-699	700 +
3.5- +						
3.0-3.4						
2.5-2.9						
2.0-2.4						
1.5-1.9						
1.0-1.4						
< 1.0						

CAT SCORES

SUCCESS EXPECTANCY TABLE FOR CAT AND GPA

	Less than 300	300-399	400-499	500-599	600-699	700 +
Succeed						
Not Succeed						

CAT SCORES

SCATTERGRAM FOR WAT AND GPA

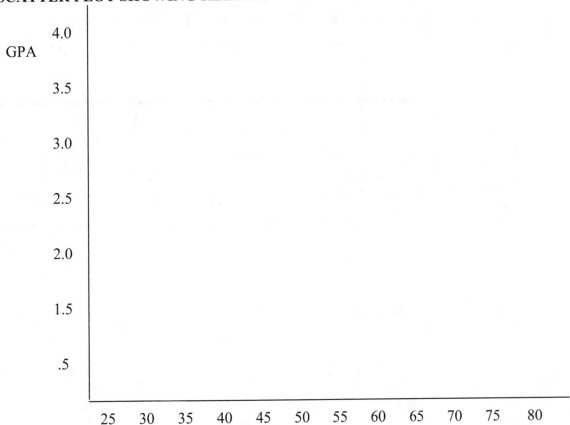

	WAT SCORES					
3.5- +						
3.0-3.4						
2.5-2.9						
2.0-2.4						
GPA 1.5-1.9						
1.0-1.4						
< 1.0						
	Less than 30	31-39	40-49	50-59	60-69	70 +

Total # of Score
Level   N=   N=   N=   N=   N=   N=

SCATTER PLOT SHOWING RELATIONSHIP OF WAT SCORES AND GPA

WAT Scores
EXPECTANCY TABLE FOR WAT AND GPA

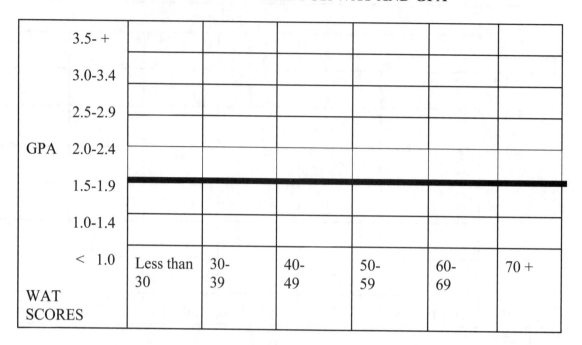

	Less than 30	30-39	40-49	50-59	60-69	70 +
3.5- +						
3.0-3.4						
2.5-2.9						
GPA 2.0-2.4						
1.5-1.9						
1.0-1.4						
< 1.0						

WAT SCORES

SUCCESS EXPECTANCY TABLE FOR WAT AND GPA

	Less than 30	30-39	40-49	50-59	60-69	70 +
Succeed						
Not Succeed						

WAT SCORES

EXERCISE 16
ADVERSE IMPACT ANALYSIS

INTRODUCTION

Legislation, policies, and testing guidelines issued by the United States government in recent years make organizations (e.g., corporations, colleges) responsible for demonstrating that their selection tests are valid, and that they do not discriminate unfairly against members of groups covered by the law. Organizations must present documented evidence that adverse impact has not occurred in selection. Adverse impact examines whether a "protected group" (e.g., women, minorities, older adults, disabled) is selected at a lower rate than another group. Adverse impact is determined by comparing the selection ratios (i.e., number of people hired divided by the number of people who apply for the job position) of different groups in a diverse pool of qualified applicants. Specifically, the "80%" rule is applied when examining adverse impact. The "80%" or "4/5" rule states that adverse impact has occurred when the minority group is selected at less than 80% of the rate at which the majority group is selected.

Let's do an example to illustrate the use of selection ratios and the "80%" rule to determine if adverse impact as occurred. If 50 White applicants are hired from a pool of 100 qualified White applicants (selection ratio = 50%), and 25 African-American applicants are hired from a pool of 100 qualified African-American applicants (selection ratio = 25%), then we can conclude that African Americans are hired at 50% of the rate at which Whites are hired. In this example, adverse impact has occurred because the African-Americans hiring rate is less than 80% of the hiring rate for White applicants.

In this exercise students will examine case study material and perform analyses to determine if the hiring procedures described have resulted in adverse impact. Analysis of adverse impact, which may or may not be the result of discrimination, is the first step in reviewing whether an organization has discriminated against a minority group.

MATERIALS NEEDED

1	Copy of Case Studies for Company A, B, and C
1	Copy of Hiring Information for Company A, B, and C
1	Adverse Impact Analysis Worksheet for Company A, B, and C

PROCEDURE

Step 1. *Form work groups.*
The class will divide into three work groups. One group will take responsibility to work with data for Company A, the second group with data for Company B, and the third group with data for Company C.

Step 2. *Review the materials.*
Each member of the group will read the assigned Case Study and the Hiring Information Table and will review the corresponding Adverse Impact Analysis Worksheet.

Step 3.   *Complete the corresponding Adverse Impact Analysis Worksheet.*
Complete the following steps for each of the 11 years represented on the Hiring Information Table.

a.   Calculate the selection ratio for the "minority group" (African-American, Female, or Older Worker) by dividing the number of people of that group that was hired by the total number of applicants from that group. Record this number in column 2 of the Worksheet.

b.   Calculate the selection ratio for the "majority group" (White, Male, or Younger Worker) by dividing the number of people of that group that were hired by the total number of applicants from that group. Record this number in column 3 of the Worksheet.

c.   For each year, divide the selection ratio (SR) of the minority group (in column 2) by the selection ratio (SR) of the majority group (in column 3). Record this number in column 4 of the Adverse Impact Analysis Worksheet. This number is the "adverse impact ratio."

Step 4.   *Assess for adverse impact.*
For each year on the Adverse Impact Analysis Worksheet, evaluate the adverse impact ratio in column 4:

a.   If the value in column 4 is less than .80, then put an "X" in the "Y" section of column 5 on the worksheet. This indicates that adverse impact in the selection process has occurred for that year.

b.   If the value in column 4 is greater than or equal to .80, then put an "X" in the "No" section of column 5 on the worksheet. This indicates that adverse impact in the selection process has not occurred for that year.

c.   Add the total number of "Xs" in each "Yes" and "No" section and put the total in the "TOTAL" row at the bottom of the worksheet. These numbers indicate the total number of years that adverse impact has and has not occurred over the past 11 years.

Step 5.   *Draw conclusions about adverse impact.*
The group will write a one-page report summarizing the results of their analysis and giving their conclusions about whether or not there is support for the discrimination case. Use the results found on the Adverse Impact Analysis Worksheet to support any conclusions.

Step 6.   *Review other Case Studies.*
All class members will review the Case Studies and Hiring Information Tables of the two companies they did not work on.

Step 7.   *Share results.*
Each group will present the results and conclusions (composed in *Step 5*) from each of the three case studies to the class.

QUESTIONS

1. Which of the three companies could be charged with practices resulting in adverse impact against a protected group? Cite data results to support your position.

2. What are some organizational issues related to biased hiring practices?

3. What are some reasons why adverse impact occurs? That is, why might a smaller percent of one group be selected compared to another group? Do these reasons necessarily mean the organization has discriminated?

CASE STUDY FOR COMPANY A

Company A has been charged with discriminatory practices in hiring its salespeople.

Specifically, the plaintiff in the race discrimination case charges that employment testing over

the past 11 years has consistently caused the over-hiring of White applicants and the under-hiring

of qualified African-American applicants. You are the human resources manager who is

evaluating the results of hiring salespeople for the last 11 years. This information is presented in

the table entitled "Hiring Information for Company A – Race." Use this information to

determine if adverse impact, with respect to race, through employment testing has occurred in

the past 11 years.

HIRING INFORMATION TABLE
FOR COMPANY A – RACE

Hiring Year	Selection Information for African Americans		Selection Information for Whites	
	Number Applied	Number Selected	Number Applied	Number Selected
2000	44	32	26	15
2001	32	11	18	6
2002	20	9	20	5
2003	22	8	19	11
2004	5	2	17	16
2005	13	8	10	8
2006	8	8	11	7
2007	13	5	12	5
2008	18	6	16	3
2009	3	2	2	2
2010	11	9	7	6

ADVERSE IMPACT ANALYSIS WORKSHEET
FOR COMPANY A – RACE

(1) Hiring Year	(2) African-American Selection Ratio (SR): # hired DIVIDED BY total African-American applicants	(3) White Selection Ratio (SR): # hired DIVIDED BY total White applicants	(4) African-American SR DIVIDED BY White SR	(5) Adverse Impact? Put an "X" in either the "Yes" or "No" column	
				Yes	No
2000					
2001					
2002					
2003					
2004					
2005					
2006					
2007					
2008					
2009					
2010					
			TOTAL		

CASE STUDY FOR COMPANY B

Company B has been charged with discriminatory practices in hiring its middle managers. Specifically, the plaintiff in the gender discrimination case charges that employment testing over the past 11 years has consistently caused the over-hiring of male applicants and the under-hiring of qualified female applicants. You are the human resources manager who is evaluating the results of hiring middle managers for the last 11 years. This information is presented in the table entitled "Hiring Information for Company B – Sex." Use this information to determine if adverse impact, with respect to gender, through employment testing has occurred in the past 11 years.

HIRING INFORMATION TABLE
FOR COMPANY B – SEX

Hiring Year	Selection Information for Females		Selection Information for Males	
	Number Applied	Number Selected	Number Applied	Number Selected
2000	12	9	14	11
2001	3	3	10	2
2002	18	2	16	10
2003	17	11	25	9
2004	18	6	13	8
2005	26	11	16	13
2006	13	3	14	9
2007	18	2	19	15
2008	8	2	6	4
2009	11	9	18	14
2010	16	4	10	4

ADVERSE IMPACT ANALYSIS WORKSHEET
FOR COMPANY B – SEX

(1) Hiring Year	(2) Female Selection Ratio (SR): # hired DIVIDED BY total female applicants	(3) Male Selection Ratio (SR): # hired DIVIDED BY total male applicants	(4) Female SR DIVIDED BY Male SR	(5) Adverse Impact? Put an "X" in either the "Yes" or "No" column	
				Yes	No
2000					
2001					
2002					
2003					
2004					
2005					
2006					
2007					
2008					
2009					
2010					
			TOTAL		

CASE STUDY FOR COMPANY C

Company C has been charged with discriminatory practices in hiring its truck drivers. Specifically, the plaintiff in the age discrimination case charges that employment testing over the past 11 years has consistently caused the over-hiring of younger worker applicants and the under-hiring of qualified older worker applicants. You are the human resources manager who is evaluating the results of hiring truck drivers for the last 11 years. This information is presented in the table entitled "Hiring Information for Company C – Age." Use this information to determine if adverse impact, with respect to age, through employment testing has occurred in the past 11 years.

HIRING INFORMATION TABLE
FOR COMPANY C – AGE

Hiring Year	Selection Information for Applicants Ages 40+[a]		Selection Information for Applicants Ages 18-30	
	Number Applied	Number Selected	Number Applied	Number Selected
2000	33	9	26	20
2001	16	5	18	15
2002	15	2	14	7
2003	22	7	18	12
2004	19	8	19	8
2005	7	7	20	11
2006	29	22	18	17
2007	21	9	10	9
2008	16	7	9	8
2009	10	4	10	5
2010	13	7	11	9

[a]Age designation of an "older worker" as being age 40 or older is based on the *Age Discrimination and Employment Act* (1967, 1978, 1986).

ADVERSE IMPACT ANALYSIS WORKSHEET
FOR COMPANY C – AGE

(1) Hiring Year	(2) Older Worker Selection Ratio (SR): # hired DIVIDED BY total older worker applicants	(3) Younger Worker Selection Ratio (SR): # hired DIVIDED BY total younger worker applicants	(4) Older worker SR DIVIDED BY Younger worker SR	(5) Adverse Impact? Put an "X" in either the "Yes" or "No" column	
				Yes	No
2000					
2001					
2002					
2003					
2004					
2005					
2006					
2007					
2008					
2009					
2010					
			TOTAL		

EXERCISE 17
INTERNAL CONSISTENCY OF THE GGAT

INTRODUCTION

Internal consistency is one of the methods used to determine the reliability of an instrument. It tries to determine whether all individual parts of an instrument measure the same construct, as does the instrument as a whole. In this exercise, you will investigate the internal consistency of the GGAT using both the split-half and the $K\text{-}R_{20}$ coefficient approaches.

MATERIALS NEEDED

1	Copy of the Correlation Data Sheet and Computation (Appendix C)
All	Copies of the results from administration of three GGAT's
1	Copy of the GGAT Scoring Worksheet
1	Copy of the GGAT Summary Sheet (two-page sheet holds data from five class members)
1	Copy of the GGAT Internal Consistency Worksheet
1+	Copies of the GGAT $K\text{-}R_{20}$ Scoring Sheet (two pages)
1	Copy of the GGAT $K\text{-}R_{20}$ Worksheet

✓ If needed, a dataset for statistical analyses is available on the accompanying CD-Rom (*Ex17-GGAT_Reliability_Data.xls*).

PROCEDURE

A. SPLIT-HALF METHOD OF DETERMINING INTERNAL CONSISTENCY

Step 1. *Gather materials.*
Each class member shall bring the three GGAT tests that they administered.

Step 2. *Score the separate halves of the tests.*
Class members will complete the GGAT Scoring Worksheet for their three participants:

    a. Place an "X" next to each question number that the participant answered correctly.

    b. Add the # right for each question for each participant, and place that number in the "All Participants" section (e.g., for Q#1, add the # right from participant #1, #2, and #3).

    c. Add the # of Xs in each column and put the answer on the "TOT" line.

    d. Compute the totals listed underneath the table.

        (1) Total GGAT for each participant

        (2) The total right of odd-numbered items for all three tests ("A" Scores)

        (3) The total right of even-numbered items for all three tests ("B" Scores)

        (4) The total right of all items for all three tests (Total GGAT Scores)

Step 3. *Record results.*
Record these results on the first line of the GGAT Summary Sheet.

Step 4. *Collate data.*
Class members will share their data with the rest of the class so that all members will have completed GGAT Summary Sheets.

Step 5. *Calculate measures of central tendency and dispersion.*
   a. On the GGAT Summary Sheet, complete the totals listed underneath the table.
   b. Using the data on the GGAT Summary Sheets, each member will compute the following for each of the three groups of scores ("A," "B," and "GGAT"):
      (1) Mean,
      (2) Variance (s^2), and
      (3) Standard Deviation (SD).
   c. Record the answers on the GGAT Internal Consistency Worksheet.

Step 6. *Calculate correlations.*
   a. Each class member will compute the Pearson Product-moment r (r_{ab}) correlation coefficient between the two halves of the test. If doing by hand, use the Correlation Data Sheet and Computation (Appendix C). Put the "Odd" (A) scores in the "X" column and the "Even" (B) scores in the "Y" column.
   b. Each class member will record the results on the GGAT Internal Consistency Worksheet.

Step 7. *Calculate correction for length.*
Compute the following Spearman-Brown Correction Formula to adjust the obtained coefficient. This corrects for test length and provides a more accurate estimate of reliability (r_{est}):

$$r_{est} = \frac{2r_{ab}}{1+r_{ab}}$$

B. **K-R $_{20}$ COEFFICIENT METHOD FOR DETERMINING INTERNAL CONSISTENCY**
Step 1. *Count right items.*
On the first three rows of the GGAT K-R$_{20}$ Scoring Sheet, class members will record the total number of their participants who answered the item correctly. This number can be obtained from the last section (i.e., "All Participants") of their GGAT Scoring Worksheet.

Step 2.   *Collate data.*
Class members will share this data with the rest of the class so that all may have completed the K-R$_{20}$ Scoring Sheets.

Step 3.   *Compute total right for the questions.*
For each question, copy the total # of participants answering correctly from the "Grand Total" box at the bottom of pages 2 and 4 of the bottom of the GGAT K-R$_{20}$ Scoring Sheet. Put this number in column 2 of the GGAT K-R$_{20}$ Worksheet.

a.   For each question, computer the total number of participants who answered correctly and place this underneath the last row of that question column on the last page of the GGAT K-R$_{20}$ Scoring Sheet. You should be computing 30 totals, one for each question.

b.   Copy this result into column 2 of the GGAT K-R$_{20}$ Scoring Sheet.

Step 4.   *Compute the number of wrong answers.*
Record the number of wrong answers to each question by subtracting the results in column 2 from the total number of GGATs being used (see GGAT Summary Sheet). Put the answers in column 4 of the GGAT K-R$_{20}$ Worksheet.

Step 5.   *Compute the proportion of persons answering correctly (p).*
Divide the number of people who answered each item correctly by the total number of GGATs being used (see GGAT Summary Sheet). Put these results in column 3 of the GGAT K-R$_{20}$ Worksheet.

Step 6.   *Compute the proportion of persons answering incorrectly (q).*
Subtract the answers to *Step 5* from 1.00. Put the results in column 5 of the GGAT K-R$_{20}$ Worksheet.

Step 7.   *Compute "pq."*
Multiply each p (Column 3) by each q (Column 5). Put the results in column 6 of the GGAT K-R$_{20}$ Worksheet.

Step 8.   *Compute the sum of pq (3pq).*
a.   Add each "*pq*" column and put the answer at the bottom of the column.

b.   Add both "*pq*" totals together to get a Grand Total ($\sum pq$).

Step 9.   Compute $K\text{-}R_{20}$.
               Use the formula below:
               n = the number of items in the total test (in this case, $n = 30$)
               s^2 = the variance of the total test (see GGAT Internal Consistency Worksheet)
               Σpq = Grand Total of pq columns

$$K - R_{20} = \frac{n}{n-1} * \frac{s^2 - \Sigma pq}{s^2}$$

Step 10.   Compute using Excel or SPSS option.
               An alternative to doing Part B steps 1-9 by hand is to do Split-half, Spearman-Brown and KR-20 reliability calculations using Excel or SPSS. Based on pilot testing with past lab students, a data file has been created for this purpose. The data file is entitled "Ex17 GGAT_Reliability_Data.xls." This data file is provided on the accompanying lab manual CD-Rom.

Step 11.   Record the data.
               Record the answer to Step 9 or Step 10 on the GGAT Internal Consistency Worksheet.

QUESTIONS

1.   Compare the results of both approaches, focusing on what information each offers with respect to reliability. Are the results similar?

2.   Discuss the rationale behind the use of the Spearman-Brown formula. Why is it important?

3.   Why might internal consistency be the method of choice for determining the reliability of instruments such as the GGAT?

GGAT SCORING WORKSHEET

Participant #1				Participant #2				Participant #3				All Participants		
Q #	R?	Q #	R?	Q #	R?	Q #	R?	Q #	R?	Q #	R?	Q #	R?	Q #	R?
01		02		01		02		01		02		01		02	
03		04		03		04		03		04		03		04	
05		06		05		06		05		06		05		06	
07		08		07		08		07		08		07		08	
09		10		09		10		09		10		09		10	
11		12		11		12		11		12		11		12	
13		14		13		14		13		14		13		14	
15		16		15		16		15		16		15		16	
17		18		17		18		17		18		17		18	
19		20		19		20		19		20		19		20	
21		22		21		22		21		22		21		22	
23		24		23		24		23		24		23		24	
25		26		25		26		25		26		25		26	
27		28		27		28		27		28		27		28	
29		30		29		30		29		30		29		30	
TOT		TOT		TOT		TOT		TOT		TOT		TOT		TOT	

Total GGAT for Participant #1 = _____   Total GGAT for Participant #2 = _____   Total GGAT for Participant #3 = _____

Total of all three "A" (Odd) Scores = _____   Total of all three "B" (Even) Scores = _____

Total of all three GGAT Scores = _____

GGAT SUMMARY SHEET

Class Member #	n	TOTAL "A" SCORES	TOTAL "B" SCORES	TOTAL GGAT SCORES	Class Member #	n	TOTAL "A" SCORES	TOTAL "B" SCORES	TOTAL GGAT SCORES
01					15				
02					16				
03					17				
04					18				
05					19				
06					20				
07					21				
08					22				
09					23				
10					24				
11					25				
12					26				
13					27				
14					28				
TOT					TOT				

n = Total # of Participants = _____   TOTAL "A" Scores = SUM of "A" + "A" = _____

TOTAL "B" Scores = SUM of "B" + "B" = _____   TOTAL "GGAT" Scores = SUM of "GGAT" + "GGAT" _____

GGAT INTERNAL CONSISTENCY WORKSHEET

Descriptive Statistics

Half Test (A):   Mean = _____ $S^2 =$ _____   SD = _____

Half Test (B):   Mean = _____ $S^2 =$ _____   SD = _____

Whole Test: Mean = _____ $S^2 =$ _____   SD = _____

Correlations

Pearson r Correlation between Halves: $r =$ ____

Spearman-Brown Corrected r: $r =$ ____

K-R$_{20}$ reliability coefficient $r =$ ____

GGAT K-R₂₀ SCORING SHEET
Page 1

QUESTION NUMBER

CLASS MEMBER #	01	02	03	04	05	06	07	08	09	10	11	12	13	14	15
TOTAL Page 1															

GGAT K-R₂₀ SCORING SHEET
Page 2

QUESTION NUMBER

CLASS MEMBER #	16	17	18	19	20	21	22	23	24	25	26	27	28	29	30
TOTAL Page 2															

GGAT K-R$_{20}$ WORKSHEET

# of People with Correct Ans. (2)	Proportion with Correct Ans. (p) (3)	# People with Incorrect Ans. (4)	Proportion with Incorrect Ans. (q) (5)	pq (3) x (5)	Item # (1)
					16
					17
					18
					19
					20
					21
					22
					23
					24
					25
					26
					27
					28
					29
					30

Sum of pq Part B =

Item # (1)	# of People with Correct Ans. (2)	Proportion with Correct Ans. (p) (3)	# People with Incorrect Ans. (4)	Proportion with Incorrect Ans. (q) (5)	pq (3) x (5)
01					
02					
03					
04					
05					
06					
07					
08					
09					
10					
11					
12					
13					
14					
15					

Sum of pq Part A =

Grand Total of $\sum pq$ = Sum pq Part A + pq Part B= _____

APPENDICES

APPENDIX A

INFORMED CONSENT FORM TEMPLATE
(AND SAMPLE IRB APPLICATION FORM)

The purpose of this testing session is to …. [explain the focus of your test – what issues will you be covering]. The entire testing process should take approximately ??? minutes.

During the testing process you will be answering questions. All testing responses of participants will be kept anonymous; a participant number will be assigned to you and your name will NOT be recorded on any testing materials.

Your participation is important and has potential benefits for this area of research [list 2-3 benefits]. There are no potential risks involved in your participation. Participation is purely voluntary, and you are free to refuse to participate or discontinue participation in this testing exercise at any time.

If you have any questions regarding your participation in the interview, feel free to contact the test administrator [your name and phone number] or the class instructor [his/her name and phone number], who will be happy to answer any questions you may have.

I have fully explained to _____ the nature and the purpose of the testing exercise and the risks involved in the testing process. I have asked if there are any questions about these procedures and have answered these questions to the best of my ability.

_____/___/_____   _____
    Date   Test Administrator's Signature

                          (____)_____
                          Test Administrator's Telephone Number

I have read the above form. The administrator has fully explained my rights and responsibilities and has answered my questions fully.

_____/___/_____   _____
    Date   Test Examinee's Signature

SAMPLE INSTITUTIONAL REVIEW BOARD (IRB) APPLICATION QUESTIONS
USED FOR APPROVAL OF RESEARCH INVESTIGATIONS
INVOLVING THE USE OF HUMAN SUBJECTS

1.   Principal Investigator _____ Faculty____ Student ____

      Department_____Tel. No./Ext._____Office No._____

      College: Arts & Sciences ____   Business & Management____   Education _____

      Co-Investigator(s)_____

2.   Title of Project_____

      _____

      Sponsor/Funding Agency_____

      Protocol/Clinical Study Identification Number _____

      Is this a multi-center study? (circle one) Yes or No   Number of Centers_____

      Total Project Period: From _____To_____

3.   Has the IRB previously reviewed this project? (circle one) Yes or No
      Review Date___/____/____

4.   Is this a project involving external support? (circle one) Yes or No

      If "yes," and the sponsor requires that a "Certification of IRB Approval" form be completed by the IRB, a copy of the sponsor's certification form must be attached to this application.

5.   Institutions involved in research:_____

6.   Does this project involve college students as subjects? (circle one) Yes or No
      If "yes," your project must have prior approval by Academic Affairs and a copy of the approval letter must be attached to this application.

7.   In your judgment does your research fall under one of the five exempt categories listed in the IRB Handbook. (circle one) Yes or No

      If you believe it does, indicate the category number under which you are claiming exemption_____

8.   Does your project fall under one of the categories eligible for expedited review? (circle one) Yes or No If so, indicate the category number _____.

9.   Description of Human Subjects: Number_____Age: ____Sex: F___M____

10.   Describe the source(s) of subjects and the selection and exclusion criteria. Specifically, where did you obtain the names of potential subjects (i.e., agency files, hospital records, local organizations, etc.)? Where and how will you contact subjects? (Attach continuation pages if needed)

11.   Costs and financial remuneration to subjects: Detail any additional costs and/or financial remuneration to subjects as a result of study participation.

12.   Give a brief description of proposed research: Include major hypotheses and research design.

13.   Procedures involving subjects: Provide a step-by-step description of each procedure, including the frequency, duration, and location.

14.   Risks: Describe the risks involved with these procedures (physical, psychological, and/or social) and the precautions you have taken to minimize these risks.

15.   Benefits: Describe the anticipated benefits to subjects, and the importance of the knowledge that may reasonably be expected to result.

16.   Protection: Describe methods for safeguarding information and for protecting subjects' rights and welfare.

17.   Informed consent: Describe the consent process and attach all consent documents to this application.

18.   I have attached to this application all supporting documents including, but not limited to: informed consent forms, questionnaire instruments, public announcements to recruit subjects, letters of approval from cooperating institutions, and one copy of external support proposal/protocol or clinical study, if applicable, etc. (circle one) Yes or No (If "no," explain below.)

PRINCIPAL INVESTIGATOR MUST SIGN THE FOLLOWING STATEMENT OF ASSURANCE:

The proposed investigation involves the use of human subjects. I am submitting this form with a description of my project prepared in accordance with institutional policy for the protection of human subjects participating in research. I understand the University's policy concerning research involving human subjects and agree to:

a.   obtain informed consent of subjects who are to participate in this project;
b.   report to the IRB any unanticipated effects on subjects that become apparent during the course of or as a result of experimentation and the actions taken as a result;
c.   cooperate with the IRB with the continuing review of this project;
d.   obtain prior approval from the IRB before amending or altering the scope of the project or implementing changes in approved consent form;
e.   maintain documentation of consent forms and progress reports as require by institutional and Federal policy.

_____

Signature of Investigator   Date

21.   Student Research: Approval by a Faculty Sponsor is required for all student research projects involving human subjects:

I affirm the accuracy of this application, and I accent the responsibility for conduct of this research and the supervision of human subjects as required by law and as documented in the IRB Handbook.

_____

Signature of Faculty Sponsor   College   Date

* * * * * * *

APPLICATION SUBMISSION

SUBMIT: the original and 6 copies of this application (omit the 6 copies if requesting exempt or expedited review)
one copy of the complete proposal/protocol/clinical study certification forms as applicable

OMIT: cover letters
investigator's vitae

SUBMIT TO: IRB Executive Secretary
Incomplete applications will be returned to the investigator.

APPENDIX B

UNIVERSAL DEMOGRAPHIC SHEET

PERSONAL DATA

ID#:_____   SEX (circle one):   M   F

Date of Birth: ___ / ___ / _____   Handedness (circle one): Left   Right   Both
              Mo   Day   Year

Relationship Status (circle one):   Single   Not single

Approximate # of hours that you exercise per week: _____

# of speeding tickets you have received: _____

EDUCATION
HIGHEST LEVEL OF EDUCATION
_____ Some high school   _____ High school diploma or GED
_____ Trade school   _____ Some college (or attending now)
_____ College degree   _____ Some graduate school (or attending now)
_____ Master's degree   _____ Advanced degree (e.g., M. D. or Ph.D.)

Major (or program of study): _____

Most recent cumulative GPA: _____

Approximate # of hours that you study (or studied) per week: _____

EMPLOYMENT
CURRENT EMPLOYMENT
_____ I am now working full time
_____ I am now working part time
_____ I am not currently working

How long have you been at your present job: _____

FIELD OF WORK
_____ Clerical   _____ Administrative
_____ Sales   _____ Health Care
_____ Social Service   _____ Computer-related
_____ Customer Service   _____ Skilled Trade
_____ Unskilled Trade   _____ Other (please list): _____

APPENDIX C

CORRELATION DATA SHEET AND COMPUTATION
CORRELATION DATA SHEET

#	X	Y	$x = (X - M_X)$	$y = (Y - M_Y)$	x^2	y^2	xy
Sum (Σ)	$\Sigma X =$	$\Sigma Y =$	$\Sigma x =$	$\Sigma y =$	$\Sigma x^2 =$	$\Sigma y^2 =$	$\Sigma xy =$

CALCULATION OF CORRELATION COEFFICIENT

1. **Symbols**

   N = # of pairs of scores $\sum$ = Sum of letters following $\sqrt{}$ = Square root

   X = Raw Score on X variable X^2 = Square of X M_X = Mean of X

   S_X = Standard Deviation of X $x = X - M_X$ x^2 = Square of x

   Y = Raw Score on Y variable M_Y = Mean of Y Y^2 = Square of Y

   S_Y = Standard Deviation of Y $y = Y - M_Y$ y^2 = Square of y

   XY = each X times corresponding Y   xy = each x times y

2. **Pearson Product Moment (*r*)**

   Steps:

   From Correlation Data Sheet

   1   a.   Complete Correlation Data Sheet

   2   b.   Apply Formula:

   $$r = \frac{\sum xy}{\sqrt{(\sum x^2)(\sum y^2)}}$$

   From Raw Data

   a.   Calculate: $\sum X$ $\sum X^2$ $(\sum X)^2$ $\sum Y$ $\sum Y^2$ $(\sum Y)^2$ $\sum XY$

   b.   Apply Formula:

   $$r = \frac{N\sum XY - \sum X \sum Y}{[\sqrt{N\sum X^2 - (\sum X)^2}] * [\sqrt{N\sum Y^2 - (\sum Y)^2}]}$$

3. **Spearman Rho (*R*)**

   Steps:

   a.   Rank X scores with highest being #1; Rank Y scores with highest being #1. Be sure to accommodate ties in value.

   b.   For each pair of ranks calculate "D" by subtracting the rank of Y from the rank of X.

   c.   Calculate D^2 by squaring each D score.

   d.   Calculate $\sum D^2$ by adding all the D^2 scores.

   e.   Apply Formula:

   $$Rho = 1 - \frac{\sum D^2}{N(N^2 - 1)}$$

APPENDIX D

COMPUTATION OF STUDENT'S *t*

1. **Symbols**

    N_X = # of scores in X group N_Y = # of scores in Y group

    Σ = Sum of whatever letters follow $\sqrt{}$ = Take square root

    X = Raw Score on X variable X^2 = Square of X

    M_X = Mean of X S_X = Standard Deviation of X

    S_X^2 = Variance of X   Y = Raw Score on Y variable

    Y^2 = Square of X M_Y = Mean of Y

    S_Y = Standard Deviation of Y S_Y^2 = Variance of Y

    s_{diff} = Standard Error of the difference between Means

2. **Steps**
    a. Calculate: ΣX ΣX ΣY ΣY^2 N_X N_Y
    b. Calculate Means of X ($\Sigma X/N$) and of Y ($\Sigma Y/N$)
    c. Calculate variances of X [$(\Sigma X^2 - (\Sigma X)^2)/N$] and of Y [$(\Sigma Y^2 - (\Sigma Y)^2)/N$]
    d. Calculate Variance of the difference between means:

        Formula:

        $$s^2_{diff} = \frac{[(N_X - 1)S_X^2] + [(N_Y - 1)S_Y^2]}{N_X + N_Y - 2} * [\frac{1}{N_X} + \frac{1}{N_Y}]$$

    e. Calculate Standard Error of the difference between means:

        Formula: $s_{diff} = \sqrt{s^2_{diff}}$

    f. Calculate *t*:

        Formula:

        $$t = \frac{M_X - M_Y}{s_{diff}}$$

    g. Look up value in Table of *t* in any statistics book.